YOUR FBI DOSSIER

John S. Helsmen

Published by
Scope International Ltd.,
62 Murray Road,
Waterlooville,
Hants PO8 9JL
Great Britain

1st Edition 1992
By John S. Helsmen

For questions and further information contact the author by mail or by fax in care of the publisher.

British Library Cataloguing in Publication Data

Helsmen, John S.
Your FBI Dossier. – (Scope Report Series)
I. Title II. Series
363.310973

ISBN 0-906619-35-1

Phototypeset by Barbara James Typesetting, Rowlands Castle, Hampshire
Printed by Hartnolls, Bodmin, Cornwall

CONTENTS

INTRODUCTION

Big brother is watching, but did you know just how closely . . . or just how well he takes notes? Even if you are not the paranoid type, the information which follows should disturb you. Summarized in this book are file descriptions of data bases maintained on a routine basis by the United States Federal Bureau of Investigation including several maintained in cooperation with the Drug Enforcement Agency and the Immigration and Naturalization Service. Their mere specifications are very revealing and their implications are more than slightly troubling.

To the government agent who will no doubt eventually read this report: Do not bristle at what herein appears to be just another irresponsible attack on the FBI and related agencies. This author has a great respect and appreciation for the dangerous and thankless work done by FBI personnel in the traditional areas of law enforcement which have always been and will always be necessary. Because of these courageous people, our world is a great deal safer from terrorists, perpetrators of all manner of violent crime, the ever more sophisticated areas of electronic fraud, and other public dangers too numerous to mention.

Issue is taken only with the abuse of power and privilege. In any organization which grows beyond a certain size and or sophistication, there are those who for whatever reason, seek to use its capabilities for their or their group's own ends. There are also those professionals who proceed with activities simply because they are fascinated by the technical challenge . . . and in the process, lose all awareness of the impact on people's lives that their actions may have.

In the case of the FBI (as well as numerous other government agencies), the political and legislative directives have long ago altered their operational charter to include many areas which are at best, only marginally in the public interest, and grossly abusive at their worst.

And finally, is the phenomenon that "mega-organizations" tend to become self-serving. This effect has nothing specifically to do with the FBI. It happens to virtually all types of large groups. Unfortunately, the FBI has long since fallen victim to the syndrome and the public suffers exceedingly for it.

In the late 1960's and early 1970's, a time when there was a great deal more public distrust of the American government in general, the issues of the right-to-privacy and secret government files caused widespread concern. It was extensively publicized that law enforcement agencies at all levels, as well as administrative departments and even intelligence gathering organizations, all kept massive data files on individuals and organizations. This data was in many cases grossly inaccurate. Furthermore, not only was it inaccessible to its subjects, its very existence was unknown to them.

No one disputed that routine record-keeping is essential to the functions of government. But, in the manner of virtually everything that it has ever attempted, the government's machinery, was misdirected into areas far afield from those originally intended. And this, very predictably, was because the data was in the hands of people with agendas of their own or of those who influenced them.

Government employees are basically ordinary people with inevitable human failings. When their supervisors tell them to do things ''for the good of the country'', they usually don't think too deeply about it. They do what they are told . . . even at the direct expense of a citizen's rights. And there was no doubt; numerous abuses were occurring daily.

Congress's response to the outcry was twofold: the Freedom of Information Act which laid down ground rules for the guarantee of public access to government files, and the Privacy Act, which requires government disclosure of what files it keeps, provides a measure of access to a subject's records, and a means to appeal and correct alleged errors.

Did the US government ''come clean'' and turn control back over to its citizens? . . . Not a chance! It is true that for some years, a backlog of requests for files were processed and a lot of needed information was disclosed. However, it soon also became evident that the Freedom of Information Act (FOIA) contained so many restrictions, that the government could (did and still does) withhold virtually anything that it wished, based on the broad authority of vaguely worded ''security'' and ''need to know'' clauses in the act.

The other favorite censorship technique in wholesale use, was to summarily claim that huge sections of the files referred to in a FOIA request, had been ''destroyed for reasons of obsolescence''. People who have followed the UFO saga will remember the incredible disappointment when in the seventies, a FOIA petition turned up only a few hundred pages of the long awaited U.S. Air Force files of Project Blue Book. Officials claimed that was all which remained. The government had several hundred people working for nearly fifteen years before they closed the files on unidentified flying objects. The arithmetic should be obvious. Some earlier estimates put the size of the orginal files at over a million pages. It started a controversy that it would take an entire book to properly address.

What had the government gained by the Freedom of Information Act? . . . a major public relations victory in the perception of the masses who rarely if ever, would want to use the rights afforded by the act. What did the public gain? . . . next to nothing. Worse, the public concern was now dissipated after the apparent victory for "freedom of information".

The Privacy Act of 1974 is not much different. Other than the psychological defenses one can put into place in the knowledge that massive files are being kept, there isn't a lot that can be done about them, or one's presence in them. To be a citizen is to be in "the system". The agencies which maintain the files in this report have virtual "carte blanche" authority to keep any records they wish. Yes, a citizen has the right to look at and appeal the content of his dossier. But, that is meaningless if the subject doesn't know his dossier exists . . . and the Act does not provide a reliable mechanism for notification when his file is created or used in some way that affects him.

Another flaw in the system is that, even if the citizen does know of his file, asks for and gets access, asks and is allowed to correct erroneous information, all the damaging information which has been already been given out, remains out and continues to cause further problems.

As you will see as you read the individual file descriptions, there are numerous exemptions from the Privacy Act. There are no explanations offered. The government simply continues to conceal what it feels to be in its best interests. In the context of an investigation to locate a fugitive murderer, a need for security is self evident. But, as will be readily apparent when you read the detail system descriptions, the role of the FBI and its intelligence gathering goes well beyond traditional law enforcement.

In the broad context of the day-to-day operations, the Bureau has no conscience about ultimate uses in its insatiable quest for information. And again, this is a product of both its highly political position in the web of American government, and its inherent self-serving nature.

The FBI has been given a great deal of leeway in its methods and policies. It must employ all its very considerable abilities to fullfill its traditional mission. But how do we prevent these same resources from being misdirected at innocent citizens? . . . Does a solution even exist? Do you view yourself caught in this electronic web? What do you yourself have at risk? You may draw your own conclusions as you read.

With note taken of these issues, we present now as a point of reference, the text of the Privacy Act of 1974, then descriptions of twelve of the FBI's records systems currently in use.

Preceding each is explanation and commentary. Following respectively, is text of the system descriptions required by law to be periodically published by each agency concerned.

Used herein is the November 26, 1990 revision, Systems of Records, as published in the Federal Register, Volume 55. No. 227, 55 FR 49146. The United States Government is solely responsible for the accuracy of those portions.

CHAPTER 1

THE PRIVACY ACT OF 1974

Officially, The Privacy Act is known as Public Law 93-579 § 3 December 1974. It appears in the United States Code as Title 5 § 552a, "Records Maintained On Individuals". It is without question, one of the most classic cases of emasculated legislation in history. No doubt its proponents really did have noble ideas in mind during its conception. But, the version that was passed is so full of exceptions and exclusions that it is essentially meaningless.

The American legislative process has evolved into a succession of reviews by committees which air objections by any and all interested parties. The concept is to confirm lengthy debate to private sessions in order not to waste the very limited time of full congressional sessions. PL 93-579 was no exception.

The Privacy Act, because it affects so many branches of government, was attacked relentlessly by a long list of agencies with vested interests. This is not at all surprising since the very nature of "disclosure" undermines everything the government is about. The text of the measures found inside reveals in no uncertain terms that numerous hard bargains were struck between the architects of the bill and its reluctant critics.

THE LEGAL MAZE

In general, we find the language of this (and virtually all other such bills for that matter) to be so convoluted and segmented as to defy comprehension by all but legal experts. If the laws of the land are to be understood, obeyed, and generally benefit the people, why are they written in such a manner that makes this practically impossible?

As a small example, in the first sentence under "definitions" we find "Agency", speaking of who this Act applies to. Agency is defined here to equate to the definition used in section (e) of the same Act. When we look in section (e), we find no definition at all. What do they really mean?

Also under definitions look at (a)(7), "routine use". Then look at (b) Conditions of Disclosure (3) routine uses. It makes reference to a still third section, (e)(4)(D) "routine uses". Typically, when references are used in this manner, it simply serves to make a text smaller or perhaps easier to read. Now . . . in the traditional method of reference assembly, watch what happens when we substitute the referred text for the reference:

> "No agency shall disclose any record . . . unless disclosure of the record would be for a routine use, the use of such record for a purpose which is compatible with the purpose for which it was collected, and subject to the requirement that the agency shall publish in the Federal Register annually a notice which shall include each routine use of the records contained in the system including the categories of users and the purpose of such use; . . . "

There actually is a technically correct line of logic inferred . . . if you can sort it out. To complicate matters further this "fragment" is part of a SINGLE SENTENCE WHICH RAMBLES ON FOR 397 WORDS BEFORE WE ENCOUNTER A PERIOD. And that would be WITHOUT incorporating the several references. Incredible!

CONDITIONS OF DISCLOSURE

Ostensibly, the purpose of this section is to protect the public against unauthorized disclosure. And as usual, at first glance, there are some sections which sound pretty good. But, any material protection is rendered totally meaningless by the provisions of the sections:

(1) Any employee of the agency who created the file.

(3) For a "routine use".

(7) Any law enforcement activity, and

(11) Any court

In other words all the entities who could really cause a problem, have free access.

And, assuming you can divine the real meaning of this legal doubletalk so liberally employed, when you read exctly what the "routine uses" are, it is immediately obvious there are no safeguard whatsoever from the abuses which really could make a difference to an individual.

The law enforcement activities alone (because they include suspicions, allegations, and affiliations with either of these two) are sufficient to remove the guarantees of privacy.

ACCESS TO RECORDS

Section (d) is the heart and soul of the Act. It is in the first two sub-sections that we find the original language of the bill's sponsors.

> "Each agency . . . upon request by any individual to gain access to his record or to any information pertaining to him which is contained in the system . . . permit him . . . to

review the record and have a copy made of all or any portion thereof in a form comprehensible to him . . .

permit the individual to request amendment of a record pertaining to him and . . .

not later than 10 days after the date of receipt of such request, acknowledge in writing such receipt; and promptly either make any correction of any portion thereof which the individual believes is not accurate, relevant, timely or complete;

or inform the individual of its refusal . . . and the reason . . . "

Not bad . . . even moderately readable. The section goes on to explain an appeal procedure that may be pursued upon an agency's refusal to grant permission to the above and if an individual disagrees.

All is well until we get to section (5). Here we find that everything becomes null and void in the event that the government happens to be in the process of preparing or "reasonably anticipates" preparing any action, adversary or otherwise, involving the subject. Quite a footnote!

AGENCY REQUIREMENTS

Here we find a great deal more of the original language of the bill. There are some genuinely good-spirited ideas having to do with relevance, minimization, accuracy, and consent. It goes on to lay down guidelines for conduct of government officials, physical security, and prior notification of changes in rules and procedures.

Then we get to a troublesome little section which begins by prohibiting any record being kept which describes how a citizen exercises his First Amendment rights. It goes on, however, to nullify this guarantee IF by chance the subject happens to be within the scope of a law enforcement activity. As we shall see later in this book, THAT could be literally thousands of things.

So again, there is no real protection where it is really needed.

CIVIL REMEDIES

In brief, you have the right to bring civil suit against the agency which denies you access, or refuses to change your record. The provisions are clear. If you win, the government pays you damages and reimburses your legal costs.

The problem is the "IF". Have you ever talked to anyone who has sued the Federal Government? These people fall in three categories: obscenely wealthy, broken and destitute from the experience, or insane. The law books are filled with notes from civil suits under the Freedom of Information Act . . . virtually all corporations. The list of individuals who have successfully brought actions against the government under the provisions of the Privacy Act is quite short by comparison.

The reason is the numerous loopholes behind which the government may hide. Again, you absolutely are guaranteed the right to sue. HOWEVER . . . keep in mind that you will be opposed by a seasoned legal army with absolutely unlimited resources.

CRIMINAL PENALTIES

This section contains a brief discussion which explains that the disclosure of information under false pretenses is a misdemeanor. Both the person who requests it and the offical who knowingly gives it out, would be held guilty.

EXCLUSIONS

The exemption section (j) is where most of the substance of the Privacy Act is nullified. The general exemption is basically that the head of any agency may, under certain criteria, exclude any system of records from the sections of the Act which authorize individual access.

Central Intelligence Agency maintained files are completely exempt without exception. For other agencies to designate a system as non-accessible, it suffices that the agency be engaged in any aspect of law enforcement or related investigation and the system be an active component of that activity.

The specific exemptions which follow are much more interesting. To begin with, any agency, upon justification, may declare any system of records exempt from all the important provisions of the act:

(c)	(3)	Notification of access by others
(d)		Access by the subject himself
(e)	(1)	Maintaining only the minimum of information
	(4)	Issuance of access procedures
(f)		Rules governing the disclosure of information to the subject.

The specific exemptions are authorized for all manner of investigative materials for law enforcement purposes . . .

EXCEPT for items which would in effect deny a citizen of his rights, privileges, or benefits under Federal law in having access to such material . . .

EXCEPT for information gathered from sources to which the Government promises to conceal their identity . . . which means virtually any informant, and anyone the government "persuaded" to reveal something.

Also excluded is any information collected pursuant to protecting the President. This gives the Secret Service carte blanche exclusion for anything they do.

The specific exclusions go on to include any kind of information which was collected relevant to personal background investigations for security clearances, employment, military service, or Federal contracts. This again applies to information where the government promises the provider that his identity would be held confidential. This is not an occasional condition, however. The standard preamble read at the beginning of a security clearance investigation interview states that the source may speak freely because his identity will not be revealed.

Another glaring item is to be found in the second sentence of the act which defines the term "individual" used in the title of the law. An "individual" is a citizen of the United States or an alien lawfully admitted for PERMANENT residence. This little exclusion obviously came from the Immigration and Naturalization camp and conveniently exempts virtually all of their applicants from ever having access to their files until or unless they succeed in their application.

CONGRESS IN PERSPECTIVE

The irony in this situation is that Congress has officially recognized the precise problems with which this author takes issue. In a subsequent section of Public Law 93-579 it states:

"The Congress finds that:

(1) The privacy of an individual is directly affected by the collection, maintenance, use, and dissemination of personal information by Federal agencies;

(2) The increasing use of computers and sophisticated information technology, while essential to the efficient operations of the Government has greatly magnified the harm to individual privacy that can occur from any collection, maintenance, use or dissemination of personal information;

(3) The opportunities for an individual to secure employment, insurance, and credit, and his right to due process, and other legal protection are endangered by the misuse of certain information;

(4) The right to privacy is a personal and fundamental right protected by the Consitution of the United States; and

(5) In order to protect the privacy of individuals identified in information systems maintained by Federal agencies, it is necessary and proper for the Congress to regulate the collection, maintenance, use, and dissemination of information by such agencies."

This is an inconvertible and accurate assessment of both the situation and the remedy. Incredibly, these words appear in the justification section of the same legislation which is discussed in this chapter.

It is absolutely bewildering that the final version of a bill could get through both the Senate and the House of Representatives with such discrepancies. The paradox set up by this noble statement of purpose and the provisions of its implementation is testimony to the state of affairs in today's Congress.

The real power in government is vested interests. This appears in the form of agencies who have evolved (or devolved) into empires . . . entities who exist only to perpetuate themselves and enhance their own power and influence . . . and then the private sector which exploits these entities to suit their own agenda.

Thus we have the public Congress, the purveyor of high sounding rhetoric, and the private Congress, a dim confused world of realities hidden as best they can by politicians who, for all the wrong reasons, daily let catastrophes become public law . . . rationalizing simply that "It is the best they can do under the circumstances, but in any case it's better than anarchy".

THE PRIVACY ACT

Read now The Privacy Act of 1974. Take note of the structure and section numbers. They will be referred to repeatedly in the chapters on information systems. The FBI and related agencies have taken full advantage of their entitlement to exemptions to the Privacy Act.

It is self-evident that more than any information systems maintained by the government, these are the ones that are potentially the most damaging and troublesome to an individual. Conversely, should the government allow them to become more accessible, it would invite a fire-storm of criticism . . . something that it is neither equipped to handle nor desires.

By their very nature, the law enforcement files are and will remain effectively closed to the public.

GOVERNMENT TEXT

PUBLIC LAW 93-579 § 3 DECEMBER 1974

"THE PRIVACY ACT OF 1974"

5 § 552a. Records maintained on individuals

(a) Definitions. – For purposes of this section –

(1) the term "agency" means agency as defined in section 552(e) of this title;

(2) the term "individual" means a citizen of the United States or an alien lawfully admitted for permanent residence;

(3) ther term "maintain" includes maintain, collect, use, or disseminate;

(4) the term "record" means any item, collection, or grouping of information about an individual that is maintained by an agency, including, but not limited to, his education, financial transactions, medical history, and crminal or employment history and that contains his name, or the identifying number, symbol, or other identifying particular assigned to the individual, such as a finger or voice print or a photograph;

(5) the term "system of records" means a group of any records under the control of any agency from which information is retrieved by the name of the individual or by some identifying number, symbol, or other identifying particular assigned to the individual;

(6) the term "statistical record" means a record in a system of records maintained for statistical research or reporting purposes only and not used in whole or in part in making any determination about an identifiable individual, except as provided by section 8 of title 13; and

(7) the term "routine use" means, which respect to the disclosure of a record, the use of such record for a purpose which is compatible with the purpose for which it was collected.

(b) Conditions of disclosure. – No agency shall disclose any record which is contained in a system of records by any means of communication to any person, or to another agency, except pursuant to a written request by, or with the prior written consent of, the individual to whom the record pertains, unless disclosure of the record would be–

(1) to those officers and employees of the agency which maintains the record who have a need for the record in the performance of their duties;

(2) required under section 552 of this title;

(3) for a routine use as defined in subsection (a)(7) of this section and described under subsection (e)(4)(D) of this section;

(4) to the Bureau of the Census for purposes of planning or carrying out a census or survey or related activity pursuant to the provisions of title 13;

(5) to a recipient who has provided the agency with advance adequate written assurance that the record will be used solely as a statistical research or reporting record, and the record is to be transferred in a form that is not individually identifiable;

(6) to the National Archives of the United States as a record which has sufficient historical or other value to warrant its continued preservation by the United States Government, or for evaluation by the Administrator of General Services or his designee to determine whether the record has such value;

(7) to another agency or to an instrumentality of any governmental jurisdiction within or under the control of the United States for a civil or criminal law enforcement activity if the activity is authorized by law, and if the head of the agency or instrumentality has made a written request to the agency which maintains the record specifying the particular portion desired and the law enforcement activity for which the record is sought;

(8) to a person pursuant to a showing of compelling circumstances affecting the health or safety of an individual if upon such disclosure notification is transmitted to the last known address of such individual;

(9) to either House of Congress, or to the extent of matter within its jurisdiction, any committee or subcommittee thereof, any joint committee of Congress or subcommittee of any such joint committee;

(10) to the Comptroller General, or any of his authorized representatives, in the course of the performance of the duties of the General Accounting Office; or

(11) pursuant to the order of a court of competent jurisdiction.

(c) Accounting of Certain Disclosures. – Each agency, with respect to each system of records under its control, shall–

(1) except for disclosures made under subsections (b)(1) or (b)(2) of this section, keep an accurate accounting of–

(A) the date, nature, and purpose of each disclosure of a record to any person or to another agency made under subsection (b) of this section; and

(B) the name and address of the person or agency to whom the disclosure is made;

(2) retain the accounting made under paragraph (1) of this subsection for at least five years or the life of the record, whichever is longer, after the disclosure for which the accounting is made;

(3) except for disclosures made under subsection (b)(7) of this section, make the accounting made under paragraph (1) of this subsection available to the individual named in the record at his request; and

(4) inform any person or other agency about any correction or notation of dispute made by the agency in accordance with subsection (d) of this section of any record that has been disclosed to the person or agency if an accounting of the disclosure was made.

(d) Access to records. – Each agency that maintains a system of records shall–

(1) upon request by any individual to gain access to his record or to any information pertaining to him which is contained in the system, permit him and upon his request, a person of his own choosing to accompany him, to review the record and have a copy made of all or any portion thereof in a form comprehensible to him, except that the agency may require the individual to furnish a written statement authorizing discussion of that individual's record in the accompanying person's presence;

(2) permit the individual to request amendment of a record pertaining to him and–

(A) not later than 10 days (excluding Saturdays, Sundays, and legal public holidays) after the date of receipt of such request, acknowledge in writing such receipt; and

(B) promptly, either–

(i) make any correction of any portion thereof which the individual believes is not accurate, relevant, timely, or complete; or

(ii) inform the individual of its refusal to amend the record in accordance with his request, the reason for the refusal, the procedures established by the agency for the individual to request a review of that refusal by the head of the agency or an officer designated by the head of the agency, and the name and business address of that official;

(3) permit the individual who disagrees with the refusal of the agency to amend his record to request a review of such refusal, and not later than 30 days (excluding Saturdays, Sundays, and legal public holidays) from the date on which the individual requests such review, complete such review and make a final determination unless, for good cause shown, the head of the agency extends such 30-day period; and if, after his review, the reviewing official also refuses to amend the record in accordance with the request, permit the individual to file with the agency a concise statement setting forth the reasons for his disagreement with the refusal of the agency, and notify the individual of the provisions for judicial review of the reviewing official's determination under subsection (g)(1)(A) of this section;

(4) in any disclosure, containing information about which the individual has filed a statement of disagreement, occurring after the filing of the statement under paragraph (3) of this subsection, clearly note any portion of the record which is disputed and provide copies of the statement and, if the agency deems it appropriate, copies of a concise statement of the reasons of the agency for not making the amendments requested, to persons or other agencies to whom the disputed record has been disclosed; and

(5) nothing in this section shall allow an individual access to any information compiled in reasonable anticipation of a civil action or proceeding.

(e) Agency requirements. – Each agency that maintains a system of records shall–

(1) maintain in its records only such information about an individual as is relevant and necessary to accomplish a purpose of the agency required to be accomplished by statute or by executive order of the President;

(2) collect information to the greatest extent practicable directly from the subject individual when the information may result in adverse determinations about an individual's rights, benefits, and privileges under Federal programs;

(3) inform each individual whom it asks to supply information, on the form which it uses to collect the information or on a separate form that can be retained by the individual–

(A) the authority (whether granted by statute, or by executive order of the President) which authorizes the solicitation of the information and whether disclosure of such information is mandatory or voluntary;

(B) the principal purpose or purposes for which the information is intended to be used;

(C) the routine uses which may be made of the information, as published pursuant to paragraph (4)(D) of this subsection; and

(D) the effects on him, if any, of not providing all or any part of the requested information;

(4) subject to the provisions of paragraph (11) of this subsection, publish in the Federal Register at least annually a notice of the existence and character of the system of records, which notice shall include–

(A) the name and location of the system;

(B) the categories of individuals on whom records are maintained in the system;

(C) the categories of records maintained in the system;

(D) each routine use of the records contained in the system, including the categories of users and the purpose of such use;

(E) the policies and practices of the agency regarding storage, retrievability, access controls, retention, and disposal of the records;

(F) the title and business address of the agency official who is responsible for the system of records;

(G) the agency procedures whereby an individual can be notified at his request if the system of records contains a record pertaining to him;

(H) the agency procedures whereby an individual can be notified at his request how he can gain access to any record pertaining to him contained in the system of records, and how he can contest its content; and

(I) the categories of sources of records in the system;

(5) maintain all records which are used by the agency in making any determination about any individual with such accuracy, relevance, timeliness, and completeness as is reasonably necessary to assure fairness to the individual in the determination;

(6) prior to disseminating any record about an individual to any person other than an agency, unless the dissemination is made pursuant to subsection (b)(2) of this section, make reasonable efforts to assure that such records are accurate, complete, timely, and relevant for agency purposes;

(7) maintain no record describing how any individual exercises rights guaranteed by the First Amendment unless expressly authorized by statute or by the individual about whom the record is maintained or unless pertinent to and within the scope of an authorized law enforcement activity;

(8) make reasonable efforts to serve notice on an individual when any record on such individual is made available to any person under compulsory legal process when such process becomes a matter of public record;

(9) establish rules of conduct for persons involved in the design, development, operation, or maintenance of any system of records, or in maintaining any record, and instruct each such person with respect to such rules and the requirements of this section, including any other rules and procedures adopted pursuant to this section and the penalties for noncompliance;

(10) establish appropriate administrative, technical, and physical safeguards to insure the security and confidentiality of records and to protect against any anticipated

threats or hazards to their security or integrity which could result in substantial harm, embarrassment, inconvenience, or unfairness to any individual on whom information is maintained; and

(11) at least 30 days prior to publication of information under paragraph (4)(D) of this subsection, publish in the Federal Register notice of any new use or intended use of the information in the system, and provide an opportunity for interested persons to submit written data, views, or arguments to the agency.

(f) Agency rules. – In order to carry out the provisions of this section, each agency that maintains a system of records shall promulgate rules, in accordance with the requirements (including general notice) of section 553 of this title, which shall–

(1) establish procedures whereby an individual can be notified in response to his request if any system of records named by the individual contains a record pertaining to him;

(2) define reasonable times, places and requirements for identifying an individual who requests his record or information pertaining to him before the agency shall make the record or information available to the individual;

(3) establish procedures for the disclosure to an individual upon his request of his record or information pertaining to him, including special procedure, if deemed necessary, for the disclosure to an individual of medical records, including psychological records, pertaining to him;

(4) establish procedures for reviewing a request from an individual concerning the amendment of any record or information pertaining to the individual, for making a determination on the request, for an appeal within the agency of an initial adverse agency determination, and for whatever additional means may be necessary for each individual to exercise fully his rights under this section; and

(5) establish fees to be charged, if any, to any individual for making copies of his record, excluding the cost of any search for and review of the record.

The Office of the Federal Register shall annually compile and publish the rules promulgated under this subsection and agency notices published under subsection (e)(4) of this section in a form available to the public at low cost.

(g) (1) Civil remedies. – Whenever any agency

(A) makes a determination under subsection (d)(3) of this section not to amend an individual's record in accordance with his request, or fails to make such review in conformity with that subsection;

(B) refuses to comply with an individual request under subsection (d)(1) of this section;

(C) fails to maintain any record concerning any individual with such accuracy, relevance, timeliness, and completeness as is necessary to assure fairness in any determination relating to the qualifications, character, rights, or opportunities of, or benefits to the individual that may be made on the basis of such record, and consequently a determination is made which is adverse to the individual; or

(D) fails to comply with any other provision of this section, or any rule promulgated thereunder, in such a way as to have an adverse effect on an individual.

the individual may bring a civil action against the agency, and the district courts of the United States shall have jurisdiction in the matters under the provisions of this subsection.

(2) (A) In any suit brought under the provisions of subsection (g)(1)(A) of this section, the court may order the agency to amend the individual's record in accordance with his request or in such other way as the court may direct. In such a case the court shall determine the matter de novo.

(B) the court may assess against the United States reasonable attorney fees and other litigation costs reasonably incurred in any case under this paragraph in which the complainant has substantially prevailed.

(3) (A) In any suit brought under the provisions of subsection (g)(1)(B) of this section, the court may enjoin the agency from withholding the records and order the production to the complainant of any agency records improperly withheld from him. In such a case the court shall determine the matter de novo, and may examine the contents of any agency records in camera to determine whether the records or

any portion thereof may be withheld under any of the exemptions set forth in subsection (k) of this section, and the burden is on the agency to sustain its action.

(B) the court may assess against the United States reasonable attorney fees and other litigation costs reasonably incurred in any case under this paragraph in which the complainant has substantially prevailed.

(4) In any suit brought under the provisions of subsection (g)(1)(C) or (D) of this section in which the court determines that the agency acted in a manner which was intentional or willful, the United States shall be liable to the individual in an amount equal to the sum of–

(A) actual damages sustained by the individual as a result of the refusal or failure, but in no case shall a person entitled to recovery receive less than the sum of $1,000; and

(B) the costs of the action together with reasonable attorney fees as determined by the court.

(5) An action to enforce any liability created under this section may be brought in the district court of the United States in the district in which the complainant resides, or has his principal place of business, or in which the agency records are situated, or in the District of Columbia, without regard to the amount in controversy, within two years from the date on whick the cause of action arises, except that where an agency has materially and willfully misrepresented any information required under this section to be disclosed to an individual and the information so misrepresented is material to establishment of the liability of the agency to the individual under this section, the action may be brought at any time within two years after discovery by the individual of the misrepresentation. Nothing in this section shall be construed to authorize any civil action by reason of any injury sustained as the result of a disclosure of a record prior to September 27, 1975.

(h) Rights of legal guardians. – For the purposes of this section, the parent of any minor, or the legal guardian of any individual who has been declared to be incompetent due to physical or mental incapacity by age by a court of competent jurisdiction, may act on behalf of the individual.

(i) **(1) Criminal penalties.** – Any officer or employee of an agency, who by virtue of his employment or official position, has possession of, or access to, agency records which contain individually identifiable information the disclosure ofwhich is prohibited by this section or by rules or regulations established thereunder, and who knowing that disclosure of the specific material is so prohibited, willfully discloses the material in any manner to any person or agency not entitled to receive it, shall be guilty of a misdemeanor and fined not more than $5,000.

(2) Any officer or employee of any agency who willfully maintains a system of records without meeting the notice requirements of subsection (e)(4) of this section shall be guilty of a misdemeanor and fined not more than $5,000.

(3) Any person who knowingly and willfully requests or obtains any record concerning an individual from an agency under false pretenses shall be guilty of a misdemeanor and fined not more than $5,000.

(j) General exemptions. – The head of any agency may promulgate rules, in accordance with the requirements (including general notice) of sections 553(b)(1), (2), and (3),(c), and (e) of this title, to exempt any system of records within the agency from any part of this section except subsections (b), (c)(1) and (2), (e)(4)(A) through (F), (e)(6), (7), (9), (10) and (11) and (i) if the system of records is–

(1) maintained by the Central Intelligence Agency; or

(2) maintained by an agency or component thereof which performs as its principal function any activity pertaining to the enforcement of criminal laws, including police efforts to prevent, control, or reduce crime or to apprehend criminals, and the activities of prosecutors, courts, correctional, probation, pardon, or parole authorities,and which consists of (A) information compiled for the purpose of identifying individual criminal offenders and alleged offenders and consisting only of identifying data and notations of arrests, the nature and disposition of criminal charges, sentencing, confinement, release, and parole and probation status; (B) information compiled for the purpose of a criminal investigation, including reports

of informants and investigators, and associated with an identifiable individual; or (C) reports identifiable to an individual compiled at any stage of the process of enforcement of the criminal laws from arrest or indictment through release from supervision.

At the time rules are adopted under this subsection, the agency shall include in the statement required under section 553(c) of this title, the reasons why the system of records is to be exempted from a provision of this section.

(k) Specific exemptions. – The head of any agency may promulgate rules, in accordance with the requirements (including general notice) of sections 553(b)(1), (2), and (3), (c), and (e) ofthis title, to exempt any system of records within the agency from subsections (c)(3), (d), (e)(1), (e)(4)(G), (H), and (I) and (f) of this section if the system of records is–

(1) subject to the provisions of section 552(b)(1) of this title;

(2) investigatory material compiled for law enforcement purposes, other than material within the scope of subsection (j)(2) of this section: *Provided, however,* That if any individual is denied any right, privilege, orbenefit that he would otherwise be entitled by Federal law, or for which he would otherwise be eligible, as a result of the maintenance ofsuch material, such material shall be provided to such individual, except to the extent that the disclosure of such material would reveal the identity of a source who furnished information to the Government under an express promises that the identity of the source would be held in confidence, or, prior to the effective date of this section, under an implied promise that the identity of the source would be held in confidence;

(3) maintained in connection with providing protective services to the President of the United States or other individuals pursuant to section 3056 of title 18;

(4) required by statute to be maintained and used solely as statistical records;

(5) investigatory material compiled solely for the purpose of determining suitability, eligibility, or qualifications for Federal civilian employment, military service, Federal contracts,or access to classified information, but only to the extent that the

disclosure of such material would reveal the identity of a source who furnished information to the Government under an express promise that the identity of the source would be held in confidence, or, prior to the effective date of this section, under an implied promise that the identity of the source would be held in confidence;

(6) testing or examination material used solely to determine individual qualifications for appointment or promotion in the Federal service the disclosure of which would compromise the objectivity or fairness of the testing or examination process; or

(7) evaluation material used to determine potential for promotion in the armed services, but only to the extent that the disclosure of such material would reveal the identity of a source who furnished information to the Government under an express promise that the identity of the source would be held in confidence, or, prior to the effective date ofthis section, under an implied promise that the identity of the source would be held in confidence.

At the time rules are adopted under this subsection, the agency shall include in the statement required under section 553(c) of this title, the reasons why the system of records is to be exempted from a provision of this section.

(*l*) **(1) Archival records.** – Each agency record which is accepted by the Administrator of General Services for storage, processing, and servicing in accordance with section 3103 of title 44 shall, for the purposes of this section, be considered to be maintained by the agency which deposited the record and shall be subject to the provisions of this section. The Administrator of General Services shall not disclose the record except to the agency which maintains the record, or under rules established by that agency which are not inconsistent with the provisions of this section.

(2) Each agency record pertaining to an identifiable individual which was transferred to the National Archives of the United States as a record which has sufficient historical or other value to warrant its continued preservation by the United States Government, prior to the effective date ofthis section, shall, for the purposes of this section, be considered to be maintained by the National Archives and shall not be

subject to the provisions of this section, except that a statement generally describing such records (modeled after the requirements relating to records subject to subsections (e)(4)(A) through (G) ofthis section) shall be published in the Federal Register.

(3) Each agency record pertaining to an identifiable individual which is transferred to the National Archives of the United States as a record which has sufficient historical or other value to warrant its continued preservation by the United States Govrnment, on or after the effective date ofthis section, shall, for the purposes of this section, be considered to be maintained by the National Archives and shall be exempt from the requirements of this section except subsections (e)(4)(A) through (G) and (e)(9) of this section.

(m) Government contractors. – When an agency provides by a contract for the operation by or on behalf of the agency of a system of records to accomplish an agency function, the agency shall, consistent with its authority, cause the requirements of this section to be applied to such system. For purposes of subsection (i) of this section any such contractor and any employee of such contractor, if such contract is agreed to on or after the effective date of this section, shall be considered to be an employee of an agency.

(n) Mailing lists. – An individual's name and address may not be sold or rented by an agency unless such action is specifically authorized by law. This provision shall not be construed to require the withholding of names and addresses otherwise permitted to be made public.

(o) Report on new systems. – Each agency shall provide adequate advance notice to Congress and the Office of Management and Budget of any proposal to establish or alter any system of records in order to permit an evaluation of the probable or potential effect of such proposal on the privacy and other personal or property rights of individuals or the disclosure of information relating to such individuals, and its effect on the preservation of the constutional principles of federalism and separation of powers.

(p) Annual report. – The President shall submit to the Speaker of the House and the President of the Senate, by June 30 of each calendar year, a consolidated report, separately listing for each Federal agency the number of records contained in any system of records which were exempted from the application of this section under the provisions of subsections (j) and (k) of this section during the preceding calendar year, and the reasons for the exemptions, and such other information as indicates efforts to administer fully this section.

(q) Effect of other laws. – No agency shall rely on any exemption contained in section 552 of this title to withhold from an individual any record which is otherwise accessible to such individual under the provisions of this section.

CHAPTER 2

JUSTICE/ATR-002

Congressional and White House Referral Correspondence Log File

This file is maintained by the Antitrust Division of the FBI and has been established to monitor correspondence between the populace and Members of Congress and the White House.

The stated purpose is to archive materials for possible future use, which may require an official response from the government. It in effect, screens and indexes letters from the public and organizations to identify any possible threat. The "uses" section is rather vague in its descriptions and tends to want to leave the impression that the information is only used in lawsuits.

The file nonetheless exists for whatever purpose. So, the next time you want to write your congressman, think twice.

Files like this one graphically portray the paranoia of the U.S. Government, and governments in general. We proudly talk of the legacy of our forefathers, Constitutional rights, the freedom of speech, assembly, and press. But just try to express a political idea that runs counter to the version of the establishment currently in vogue . . . and wham!

The FBI calls it sedition, a serious federal offense. The laws were passed to prevent anarchy, which most would agree, is just as bad as totalitarianism. They are being used, however, to maintain a rather strict status quo. How quickly we forget that Jefferson, Franklin, Madison, et. al. were some of the greatest masters of sedition in history . . . and the powers that advocated THEIR repression lost because they lost the confidence of the people. The difference now is that the government is using high technology to aid their monitoring of the masses. Nonetheless, given enough time, history does tend to repeat.

If you have something complementary to say to your congressman, go ahead and write if you must. On the other hand, caution is still recommended. If HE ever comes under fire for some scandal, all his past and present supporters will be scrutinized and/or harrassed. If you are writing to criticize, special prudence is advised. You could well wind up on a list of potential sedition suspects. Note also the record retention life . . . indefinite.

GOVERNMENT TEXT

JUSTICE/ATR-002

SYSTEM NAME: Congressional and White House Referral Correspondence Log File.

SYSTEM LOCATIONS:

U.S. Department of Justice;
10th & Constitution Avenue, NW
Washington, DC 20530.

CATEGORIES OF INDIVIDUALS COVERED BY THE SYSTEM:

Present and former members of Congress, and citizens whose correspondence is received directly or referred by members of Congress or Congressional or White House staff.

CATEGORIES OF RECORDS IN THE SYSTEM:

This system contains an index record to correspondence from citizens, present and former members of the Congress and White House staff.

AUTHORITY FOR MAINTENANCE OF THE SYSTEM:

Authority for the establishment and maintenance of this system exists under 44 U.S.C. 301 and 5 U.S.C. 301.

PURPOSES(S):

The purpose of this system is to enable Antitrust Division personnel to monitor responses and identify other material related to citizen inquiries and inquiries or referrals by members or committees of the Congress and by the White House staff.

ROUTINE USES OF RECORDS MAINTAINED IN THE SYSTEM, INCLUDING CATEGORIES OF USERS AND THE PURPOSES OF SUCH USES:

A record maintained in this system, or any facts derived therefrom, may be disseminated in a proceeding before a court or adjudicative body before which the Antitrust Division is authorized to appear, when

(1) the Antitrust Division, or any subdivision thereof; or

(2) any employee of the Antitrust Division in his or her official capacity; or

(3) any employee of the Antitrust Division in his or her individual capacity where the Department of Justice has agreed to represent the employee; or

(4) the United States, or any agency or subdivision thereof; or

(5) the United States,

where the Antitrust Division determines that the litigation is likely to affect it or any of its subdivisions, is a party to litigation and such records are determined by the Antitrust Division to be arguably relevant to the litigation.

Release of information to the news media: Information permitted to be released to the news media and the public pursuant to 28 CFR 50.2 may be made available from systems of records maintained by the Department of Justice unless it is determined the release of the specific information in the context of a particular case would constitute an unwarranted invasion of personal privacy.

Release of information to Members of Congress. Information contained in systems of records maintained by the Department of Justice, not otherwise required to be released pursuant to 5 U.S.C. 552, may be made available to a Member of Congress or staff acting upon the Member's behalf when the Member or staff requests the information on behalf of and at the request of the individual who is the subject of the record.

Release of information to the National Archives and Records Administration (NARA) and to the General Services Administration (GSA): A record from a system of records may be disclosed as a routine use to NARA and GSA in records management inspections conducted under the authority of 44 U.S.C. 2904 and 2906.

POLICIES AND PRACTICES FOR STORING, RETRIEVING, ACCESSING, RETAINING, AND DISPOSING OF RECORDS IN THE SYSTEMS:

STORAGE:

Paper documents are stored in looseleaf binders and file folders; abbreviated or summarized information is stored in a computerized tracking system.

RETRIEVABILITY:

Inquiry and response documents are retrieved by date or through manual and automated indexes which are accessed by name, subject matter, control number, etc., Summary data on inquiries received prior to March 7, 1983, is retrieved from the manual index cards; as of March 7, 1983, a summary data is retrieved from magnetic disks and tapes. Summary data consists of data elements as Congressional Member or constituent name, subject matter, date of inquiry, date assigned, date of response, etc.

SAFEGUARDS:

Information contained in the system is unclassified.

During working hours access to the system is controlled and monitored by Antitrust division personnel in the area where the system is maintained; during non-duty hours all doors to such area are locked. In addition only Antitrust Division personnel who have a need for the information contained in the system have the appropriate password for access to the system.

RETENTION AND DISPOSAL: Indefinite.

SYSTEM MANAGER(S) AND ADDRESS:

Chief, Legislative Unit: Antitrust Division
U.S. Department of Justice
10th & Constitution Avenue, NW
Washington, DC 20530

NOTIFICATION PROCEDURE:

Address inquiries to:

The Assistant Attorney General
Antitrust Division
Department of Justice
10th & Constitution Avenue, NW
Washington, DC 20530.

RECORD ACCESS PROCEDURES:

Requests for access for a record from this system shall be written and clearly identified as "Privacy Access Request". The request should include the name of the member of Congress or White House staff originating a request or referral and the date thereof. Requester should indicate a return address.

CONTESTING RECORD PROCEDURES:

Individuals desiring to contest or amend information maintained in the system should state clearly and concisely what information is being contested, the reasons for contesting it and the proposed amendment to the information sought.

RECORD SOURCE CATEGORIES:

Source of information maintained in the system are those records reflecting inquiries or referrals of citizen correspondence by present and former members of Congress or White House staff.

SYSTEMS EXEMPTED FROM CERTAIN PROVISIONS OF THE ACT: None.

CHAPTER 3

JUSTICE/CRM-012
Organized Crime and Racketeering Section, General Index File and Associated Records.

This file is maintained by the Criminal Division of the FBI. It, as its name implies, is a collection of data relating to all activities in the realms of organized crime. This is all well and good until we get to the next part, ''persons alleged to be involved . . . and those alleged to be associated with those alleged to be involved''. Now we're getting to the real essence of investigative law, universal suspicion.

A person can land in the file by having been implicated by a third party rightly or wrongly.. and once in, you're in, as we shall shortly see. As you can imagine, with no concrete evidence required, this could be virtually anyone.

Under the category of ''Uses of the Information'', we again find the expected items regarding investigation and prosecution. Then buried down in the middle of the section, we find noted that information can be given to an actual or potential party or his attorney for the purpose of negotiation or discussion on such matters as settlement of the case or matter, plea bargaining, or ''informal'' discovery proceedings. What this translates to is a license to "persuade" a citizen to do, provide, or testify to, whatever suits the Bureau's purposes.

This is a very touchy subject. No government official will admit to use of the practice of ''strong-arming''. It happens nonetheless. Not only the Bureau, but numerous other Federal and local agencies routinely use carefully edited information combined with fear, to intimidate citizens into cooperating in furtherance of their purposes, honorable or not.

We see also, that the information can be disseminated to an endless list of other agencies for law enforcement purposes. But also, it can be given out to influence decisions regarding employment by the government, government contracts, issuances of licenses, grants or any other benefits over which the government has influence. This authority is particularly prone to abuses. The government can in effect, based on totally unsubstantiated information, eliminate a citizen's access to some or all of his rightful entitlements, and in the realm of commerce, put him out of business.

Under ''Retention and Disposal'' we find that the records have an indefinite life. This problem speaks for itself.

Under "Record Access Procedures" we are told that the major part of the system is exempt from the access requirements of the Act. It goes on to say that one may make a request in the domain which is not specifically exempt, and then the FBI will make an individual determination as to whether access will be allowed. This means that, if the FBI has no proceedings active or contemplated concerning the subject, they will "consider" the request.

Under "Contesting Record Procedures", we discover that, you may submit a request for correction, but the system is exempt from the contesting provisions of the Act.

In summary, we have an obviously necessary system, whose utility to the public interest cannot be questioned. But at the same we must unavoidably conclude that its guidelines for use and imposed secrecy make it extremely prone to abuse that same public.

GOVERNMENT TEXT

JUSTICE/CRM-012

SYSTEM NAME: Organized Crime and Racketeering Section, General Index File and Associated Records

SYSTEM LOCATION:

U.S. Department of Justice
Criminal Division, Organized Crime and Racketeering Section
10th Street and Constitution Avenue NW
Washington, DC 20530.

CATEGORIES OF INDIVIDUALS COVERED BY THE SYSTEM:

Persons who have been prosecuted or are under investigation for potential or actual criminal prosecution as well as persons allegedly involved in organized criminal activity and those alleged to be associated with the subject.

CATEGORIES OF RECORDS IN THE SYSTEM:

The system consists of alphabetical indices bearing individual names and the associated records to which they relate, arranged either by subject matter or individual identifying number, of all incoming correspondence, cases, matters, investigations, and memoranda assigned, referred, or of interest, to the {PG 49148} Organized Crime and Racketeering Section. The records in this system concern matters primarily involving organized crime and include, but are not limited to, case files; investigative reports; intelligence reports; subpoena and grand jury files; records of warrants and electronic surveillances; records of indictment, prosecution, conviction, parole, probation, or immunity; legal papers; evidence; exhibits; items classified confidential, secret, and top secret; and various other files related to the Sections activities and it ongoing investigations, prosecutions, cases, and matters. Records concerning subject matters described in this system may also be contained in JUSTICE/CRM- 0012.

AUTHORITY FOR MAINTENANCE OF THE SYSTEM:

This system is established and maintained pursuant to 44 U.S.C. 3101 and the Presidential Directive on the Federal Drive Against Organized Crime, issued May 5, 1966 (Weekly Compilation of Presidential Documents, Vol. 2, W. No. 18 (1966)). In addition, this system is maintained to assist in implementing and enforcing the criminal laws of the United States, particularly those codified in title 18, United States Code. This system is also maintained to implement the provisions codified in 28 CFR .55 particularly subsection (g).

ROUTINE USES OF RECORDS MAINTAINED IN THE SYSTEM, INCLUDING CATEGORIES OF USERS AND THE PURPOSES OF SUCH USES:

A record maintained in this system of records may be disseminated as a routine use of such record as follows:

(1) In any case in which there is an indication of a violation or potential violation of law, whether civil, criminal, or regulatory in nature, the record in question maybe disseminated to the appropriate federal, state, local, or foreign agency charged with the responsibility for investigating or prosecuting such violation or charged with enforcing or implementing such law;

(2) In the course of investigating the potential or actual violation of any law, whether civil, criminal, or regulatory in nature, or during the course of a trial or hearing or the preparation for a trial or hearing for such violation, a record may be disseminated to a federal, state, local, or foreign agency, or to an individual, or organization, if there is reason to believe that such agency, individual, or organization possesses information relating to the investigation, trial, or hearing and the dissemination is reasonably necessary to elicit such information or to obtain the cooperation of a witness or an informant;

(3) A record relating to a case or matter may be disseminated in an appropriate federal, state, local, or foreign court or grand jury proceeding in accordance with established constitutional, substantive, or procedural law or practice;

(4) A record relating to a case or matter may be disseminated to a federal, state, or local administrative or regulatory proceeding or hearing in accordance with the procedures governing such proceeding or hearing;

(5) A record relating to a case or matter may be disseminated to an actual or potential party or his attorney for the purpose of negotiation or discussion on such matters as settlement of the case or matter, plea bargaining, or informal discovery proceedings;

(6) A record relating to a case or matter that has been referred by an agency for investigation, prosecution, or enforcement, or that involves a case or matter within the jurisdiction of an agency, may be disseminated to such agency to notify the agency of the status of the case or matter or of any decision or determination that has been made, or to make such other inquiries and reports as are necessary during the processing of the case or matter;

(7) A record relating to a person held in custody pending or during arraignment, trial, sentence, or extradition proceedings, or after conviction or after extradition proceedings, may be disseminated to a federal, state, local, or foreign prison, probation, parole, or pardon authority, or to any other agency or individual concerned with the maintenance, transportation, or release of such a person;

(8) A record relating to a case or matter may be disseminated to a foreign country pursuant to an international treaty or convention entered into and ratified by the United States or to an executive agreement;

(9) A record may be disseminated to a federal, state, local, foreign, or international law enforcement agency to assist in the general crime prevention and detection efforts of the recipient agency or to provide investigative leads to such agency;

(10) A record may be disseminated to a federal agency, in response to its request, in connection with the hiring or retention of an employee, the issuance of a security clearance, the reporting of an investigation of an employee, the letting of a contract, or the issuance of a license, grant, or other benefit by the requesting agency, to the extent that the information relates to the requesting agency's decision on the matter;

(11) A record may be disseminated to the public, news media, trade association, or organized groups, when the purpose of the dissemination is educational or informational, such as descriptions of crime trends or distinctive or unique modus operandi, provided that the record does not contain an information identifiable to a specific individual other than such modus operandi;

(12) A record maybe disseminated to a foreign country, through the United States Department of State or directly to the representative of such country, to the extent necessary to assist such country in apprehending and/or returning a fugitive to a jurisdiction which seeks his return;

(13) A record that contains classified national security information and material may be disseminated to persons who are engaged in historical research projects, or who have previously occupied policy making provisions to which they were appointed by the President, in accordance with the provisions codified in 28 CFR 17.60.

Information may be released to the news media and the public pursuant to 28 CFR 50.2 unless it is determined that release of the specific information in the context of a particular case would constitute an unwarranted invasion of personal privacy.

Information may be made available to a Member of Congress or staff acting upon the Member's behalf when the Member or staff requests the information on behalf of and at the request of the individual who is the subject of the record; and a record may be released to the National Archives and Records Administration and to the General Services Administration in records management inspections conducted under the authority of 44 U.S.C. 2904 and 2906.

POLICIES AND PRACTICES FOR STORING, RETRIEVING, ACCESSING, RETAINING, AND DISPOSING OF RECORDS IN THE SYSTEM:

STORAGE:

The records in this sytem are stored on various documents, tapes, disc packs, and punch cards, some of which are contained in files, on index cards, or in related type materials.

RETRIEVABILITY:

The system is accessed by name but may be grouped for the conveninence of the user by subject matter, e.g., parole file, photograph file, etc.

SAFEGUARDS:

Materials related to the system are maintained in appropriately restricted areas and are safeguarded and protected in accordance with applicable Department rules.

RETENTION AND DISPOSAL:

Currently there are no provisions for the disposal of the records in the system.

SYSTEM MANAGER(S) AND ADDRESS:

Assistant Attorney General

Criminal Division, U.S. Department of Justice

10th Street and Constitution Avenue NW.

Washington, DC 20530.

NOTIFICATION PROCEDURE:

Inquiry concerning the system should be addressed to the System Manager listed above.

RECORD ACCESS PROCEDURES:

The major part of this system is exempted from this requirement under 5 U.S.C. 552a(j)(2), (k)(1), or (k)(2). To the extent that this system of records is not subject to exemption, it is subject to access and contest. A determination as to exemption shall be made at the time a request for access is received. A request for access to a record contained in this system shall be made in writing, with the envelope and the letter clearly marked ''Privacy Access Request''. Include in the request the name of the individual involved, his birth date and place, or any other identifying number or information which may be of assistance in locating the record, the name and of the case or matter involved, if known, and the name of the judicial district involved, if known. The requestor will also provide a return address for transmitting the information. Access requests will be directed to the system manager listed above. Records in this system are exempt from the access provisions of the Act in accordance with the applicable exemption notice.

CONTESTING RECORD PROCEDURES:

Individuals desiring to contest or amend information maintained in the system should direct their request to the system manager listed above, stating clearly and concisely what information is being contested, the reasons for contesting it, and the proposed amendment to the information sought. Records in this system are exempt from the contesting provisions of the Act in accordance with the applicable exemption notice.

RECORD SOURCE CATEGORIES:

1. Federal, state, local, or foreign government agencies concerned with the administration of criminal justice and non-law enforcement agencies both public and private
2. Members of the public
3. Government employees
4. Published material
5. Witnesses and informants

SYSTEMS EXEMPTED FROM CERTAIN PROVISIONS OF THE ACT:

The Attorney General has exempted this system from subsections (c)(3) and (4), (d), (e)(1), (2) and (3), (e)(4)(G), (H), and (I), (e)(5), and (8), (f), and (g) of the Privacy Act pursuant to 5 U.S.C. 552a (j)(2). Rules have been promulgated in accordance with the requirements of 5 U.S.C. 553(b), (c), and (e) and have been published in the Federal Register.

CHAPTER 4

JUSTICE/JMD-016
Employee Assistance Program Treatment and Referral Records

This file is internal to the Bureau, but serves as a good example of how a database can be double edged. It contains clinical records of FBI employees, former employees, and family members. Its principle use is in the execution of the counseling and rehabilitation function of the Employee Assistance Program.

After a treatment program has been embarked upon or has finished, however, the records may come back to haunt the subject in the form of disciplinary actions within the bureau, or a report filed with local police authorities if in the course of treatment, a counsellor discovers something which he believes is illegal.

Ironically, though this system is subject to the benefits of The Privacy Act, as soon as some adversary proceeding is initiated, the record suddenly becomes inaccessible under the ''law enforcement'' exemptions.

The one ray of hope with this file is that the life-span is only three years, after which the records are shredded. Apparently, the FBI tends to regard its own as a different class of citizen entitled to more civil rights protection.

GOVERNMENT TEXT

JUSTICE/JMD- 016

SYSTEM NAME: Employee Assistance Program Treatment and Referral Records

SYSTEM LOCATION:

Justice Management Division
Department of Justice
10th St. & Constitution Avenue, NW
Washington, DC 20530.

CATEGORIES OF INDIVIDUALS COVERED BY THE SYSTEM:

Current and former employees of the Offices, Boards and Divisions and, upon occasion, of the Bureaus of the Department (as listed at 28 CFR 0.1); United States Attorney organizations; and the Office of Justice Programs of the Department of Justice who have sought counseling or been referred to or for treatment through the EAP. To the limited degree that treatment and referral may be provided to family members of these employees, these individuals, too, may be covered by the system.

CATEGORIES OF RECORDS IN THE SYSTEM:

The system contains records of employees (and in limited cases, employee family members) who have sought or been referred to the EAP for treatment or referral. Examples of data found in such records include:

* Notes and documentation of internal EAP counseling
* Records of treatment and counseling referrals,
* Records of employee attendance at treatment and counseling programs
* Prognosis or treatment information
* Documents received from supervisors or personnel on work place problems or performance
* Home addresses and/or phone numbers
* Insurance data

* Supervisors' phone number
* Addresses of treatment facilities or individuals providing treatment
* Leave records
* Written consent forms and abeyance agreements (see below)
* Information on confirmed unjustified positive drug tests
* Results from EAP treatment drug tests
* Identification data, such as sex, job title and series, and date of birth.

AUTHORITY FOR MAINTENANCE OF THE SYSTEM:

42 U.S.C. 290dd, et seq. and 290ee, et seq.; 42 CFR Sec. 2, et seq.; Executive Order 12564, 5 U.S.C. 3301 and 7901; 44 U.S.C. 3101 and Pub. L. No. 100- 71, Sec. 503 (July 11, 1937).

PURPOSE:

These records are to be used by EAP personnel in the execution of the counseling and rehabilitation function. They document the nature and effects of employee problems and counseling by the EAP and referral to, and progress and participation in, outside treatment and counseling programs and the rehabilitation process. These records may also be used to track compliance with agreements made to mitigate discipline based upon treatment (abeyance agreements).

ROUTINE USES OF RECORDS MAINTAINED IN THE SYSTEM, INCLUDING CATEGORIES OF USERS AND PURPOSES OF SUCH USES:

In addition to those disclosures permitted by the Privacy Act itself, fn 15 U.S.C. 552a(b), permissive disclosures, without individual consent, are as follows:

To the extent that release of alcohol and drug abuse records is more restricted than other records subject to the Privacy Act, JMD will follow such restrictions: (See 42 U.S.C. 290dd and 290ee)

(a) To report, under State law, incidents of suspected child abuse or neglect to appropriate State or local authorities.

(b) To the extent necessary to prevent an imminent and potential crime which directly threatens loss of life or serious bodily injury.

CONTESTING RECORDS PROCEDURES:

Direct all requests to contest or amend information to the system manager identified above. The request should follow the record access procedure, listed above, and should state clearly and concisely the information being contested, the reason for contesting it, and the proposed amendment thereof. Clearly mark the envelope "Freedom of Information Act/Privacy Act Request."

RECORD SOURCE CATEGORIES:

Records are generated by EAP personnel, referral counseling and treatment programs or individuals, the employee who is the subject of the record, personnel office and the employee's supervisor. In the case of drug abuse counseling, records may also be generated by the staff of the Drug-Free Workplace Program and the Medical Review Officer. {PG 49150}

POLICIES AND PRACTICES FOR STORING, RETRIEVING, ACCESSING, RETAINING, AND DISPOSING OF RECORDS IN THE SYSTEM:

STORAGE:

All records are stored in paper folders in locked file cabinets in accordance with 42 CFR 2.16.

RETRIEVABILITY:

Records are indexed and retrieved by identifying number or symbol, cross-indexed to employee names.

SAFEGUARDS:

Records are kept in a secure room in locked file cabinets. Only the EAP Administrator or a designated staff member will access or disclose the records.

RETENTION AND DISPOSAL:

Records are retained for three years after the individual ceases contact with the counselor unless a longer retention period is necessary because of pending administrative or judicial procedings. In such cases, the records are retained for six months after the case is closed. Records are destroyed by shredding or burning.

SYSTEM MANAGER AND ADDRESS:

Director, Employee, Assistance Programs
Justice Management Division
Department of Justice
10th St. & Constitution Avenue, NW.
Washington, D.C. 20530.

NOTIFICATION PROCEDURE:

Address all inquiries to the system manager.

RECORD ACCESS PROCEDURES:

Make all requests for access in writing to the system manager identified above. Clearly mark the envelope and letter ''Freedom of Information Act/Privacy Act Requests.'' Provide the full name and notarized signature of the individual who is the subject of the record, the dates during which the individual was in counseling, any other information which may assist in identifying and locating the record, and a return address.

SYSTEM EXEMPTED FROM CERTAIN PROVISIONS OF THE ACT: None

CHAPTER 5

JUSTICE/FBI-001
National Crime Information Center (NCIC)

The NCIC system is the most well known and widely used of FBI files. It is actually a network of systems which are roughly divided into persons or things that are "wanted", criminal history (CCH), and some special categories like Secret Service and the Federal Marshall's Witness security programs.

The "things" that are wanted can be virtually anything, but special categories exist for guns, license plates, vehicles, boats, and securities. The "persons" category is made up of a number of sub-files such as of course, criminals, but also missing persons, juveniles, and unidentified persons (or body parts). There is a special category for Canadian warrants.

Most of the data is collected by the nation's police services and gathered in this system. Thus, the FBI NCIC serves as a clearinghouse for law enforcement information. This amazingly large computer database is connected to an on-line network to all levels of law enforcement organizations around the United States, its possessions, Canada, and selected locations outside. With it, any police agency can know what virtually any other has done concerning any criminal matter.

With regard to its various "want" files, except for the records generated internally, the FBI relies on the agency which originated the record, to clear it. There are some record-life limitations detailed later in the government text, which govern how this part of the system is maintained.

The NCIC is a day-to-day working tool of all law enforcement agencies. Some records, like stolen vehicles without ID numbers, are cleared after only 90 days. Stolen travelers checks are cleared automatically after two years, etc. The concept is to maintain a relatively streamlined system which retains only current useable information.

The bad news, is the exemption from disclosure and correction provisions of the Privacy Act. There is an alternate procedure given, but it is somewhat ludicrous. To see your record, you must go in person to the local police agency who originated your record, and be fingerprinted to ascertain your identity. If the object of your query was to find out IF you were "wanted", you might get to see more than just your record.

This is the file, incidentally, that is consulted when you ask your local police for a "good conduct certificate". It is also queried when you are stopped for any routine traffic violation (patrol cars are now commonly equipped with computers on radio-link), and when you come to the notice of the government for any one of a wide variety of fairly ordinary reasons. This includes applications for and renewals of passports, government employment, and on the discretion of any official, processing an application for virtually any government benefit. It also feeds the famous "watch file" maintained by the State Department for monitoring by immigration officers.

A number of rather elaborate security measures are in place for this system. This is necessary because of the large number of people outside the FBI who have access. And as such, it is more at risk to unauthorized access than other FBI systems. Security is only as good as the integrity of local police personnel. There is however, an internal computer log which keeps track of ALL access or attempted access from anywhere for any purpose. If they have a problem with leakage of information, there is a trail with which to find the leak.

The system has been around for many years and is technically and administratively mature. As one would expect with a system of this size and complexity, the NCIC is open to abuse. But on balance, because it is for the most part maintained by and used by local law enforcement, it does far more good than bad with respect to the general public. It is also the principal reason that one need have a healthy respect for the efficiency of law enforcement at all levels. The perils for those who are at odds with the law, exist in all locations of the country at once as a result of high tech communications.

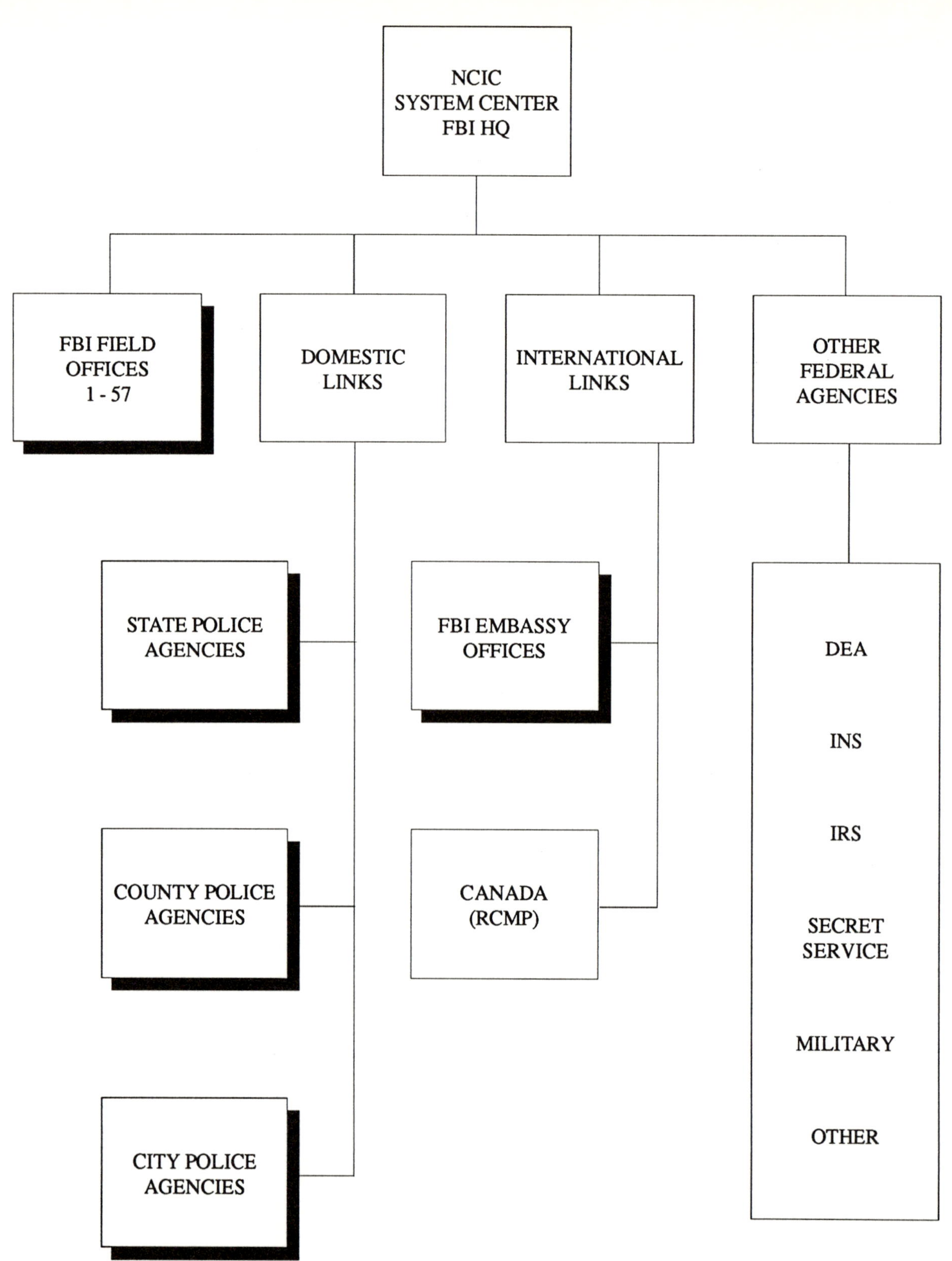

FIGURE 5-1 Schematic of NCIC Computer Network

GOVERNMENT TEXT

JUSTICE/FBI 001

SYSTEM NAME: National Crime Information Center (NCIC).

SYSTEM LOCATIONS:

Federal Bureau of Investigation
J. Edgar Hoover Bldg.
10th and Pennsylvania Avenue NW.
Washington, D.C. 20535

CATEGORIES OF INDIVIDUALS COVERED BY THE SYSTEM:

A. Wanted Persons:

1. Individuals for whom Federal warrants are outstanding.
2. Individuals who have committed or have been identified with an offense which is classified as a felony or serious misdemeanor under the existing penal statutes of the jurisdictions originating the entry and felony or misdemeanor warrant has been issued for the individual with respect to the offense which was the basis of the entry. Probation and parole violators meeting the foregoing criteria.
3. A "Temporary Felony Want" may be entered when a law enforcement agency has need to take prompt action to establish a "want" entry for the apprehension of a person who has committed, or the officer has reasonable grounds to believe has committed, a felony and who may seek refuge by fleeing across jurisdictionary boundaries and circumstances preclude the immediate procurement of a felony warrant. A "Temporary Felony Want" shall be specifically identified as such and subject to verification and support by a proper warrant within 48 hours following the initial entry of a temporary want. The agency originating the "Temporary Felony Want" shall be responsible for subsequent verification or re-entry of a permanent want.
4. Juveniles who have been adjudicated delinquent and who have escaped or absconded from custody, even though no arrest warrants were issued. Juveniles who have been charged with the commission of a delinquent act that would be a crime if committed by an adult, and who have fled from the state where the act was committed.

5. Individuals who have committed or have been identified with an offense committed in a foreign country, which would be a felony if committed in the United States, and for whom a warrant of arrest is outstanding and for which act an extradition treaty exists between the United States and that country.

6. Individuals who have committed or have been identified with an offense committed in Canada and for whom a Canada-Wide Warrant has been issued which meets the requirements of the Canada-U.S. Extradition Treaty, 18 U.S.C. 3184.

B. Individuals who have been charged with serious and/or significant offenses.

C. Missing Persons:

1. A person of any age who is missing and who is under proven physical/mental disability or is senile, thereby subjecting himself or others to personal and immediate danger.

2. A person of any age who is missing under circumstances indicating that his disappearance was not voluntary.

3. A person of any age who is missing under circumstances indicating that his physical safety is in danger.

4. A person who is missing and declared unemancipated as defined by the laws of his state of residence and does not meet any of the entry criteria set forth in 1, 2, or 3 above.

D. Individuals designated by the U.S. Secret Service as posing a potential danger to the President and/or other authorized protectees.

E. Unidentified Persons:

1. Any unidentified deceased person.

2. Any person who is living and unable to ascertain his/her identity (e.g., infant, amnesia victim).

3. Any unidentified catastrophe victim.

4. Body parts when a body has been dismembered.

CATEGORIES OF RECORDS IN THE SYSTEM:

A. Stolen Vehicle File:

1. Stolen vehicles.
2. Vehicles wanted in conjunction with felonies or serious misdemeanors.
3. Stolen vehicle parts, including certificates of origin or title.

B. Stolen License Plate File:

1. Stolen or missing license plate.

C. Stolen/Missing Gun File:

1. Stolen or missing guns.
2. Recovered guns, when ownership of which has not been established.

D. Stolen Article File

E. Wanted Persons File: Described in "CATEGORIES OF INDIVIDUALS COVERED BY THE SYSTEM: A. Wanted Persons."

F. Securities File:

1. Serially numbered stolen, embezzled, counterfeited, missing securities.
2. "Securities" for present purposes of this file are currency (e.g., bills, bank notes) and those documents or certificates which generally are considered to be evidence of debt (e.g., bonds, debentures, notes) or ownership of property (e.g., common stock, preferred stock), and documents which represent subscription rights, warrants and which are of those types trades in the securities exchanges in the United States, except for commodities futures. Also included are warehouse receipts, travelers checks and money orders.

G. Stolen Boat File

H. Computerized Criminal History File: A cooperative Federal-state program for the interstate exchange of criminal history record information for the purpose of facilitating the interstate exchange of such information among criminal justice agencies.

I. Missing Person File: Described in "CATEGORIES OF INDIVIDUALS COVERED BY THE SYSTEM: C. Missing persons."

J. U.S. Secret Service Protective File: Described in "CATEGORIES OF INDIVIDUALS COVERED BY THE SYSTEM: D."

K. Identification records regarding persons enrolled in the United States Marshals Service Witness Security Program who have been charged with serious and/or significant offenses: Described in "CATEGORIES OF INDIVIDUALS COVERED BY THE SYSTEM: B."

L. Foreign Fugitive File: Identification data regarding persons who are fugitives from foreign countries, who are described in "CATEGORIES OF INDIVIDUALS COVERED BY THE SYSTEM: A. Wanted Persons, 5."

M. Canadian Warrant File: Identification data regarding Canadian wanted persons who are described in "CATEGORIES OF INDIVIDUALS COVERED BY THE SYSTEM: A. Wanted Persons, 6."

N. Unidentified Person File: Described in "CATEGORIES OF INDIVIDUALS COVERED BY THE SYSTEM: E." Unidentified Persons.

AUTHORITY FOR MAINTENANCE OF THE SYSTEM:

The system is established and maintained in accordance with 28 U.S.C. 534; Department of Justice Appropriation Act, 1973, Pub. L. 92-544, 86 Stat. 1115, Securities Acts Amendment of 1975, Pub. L. 94-29, 89 Stat. 97; and Exec. Order No. 10450, 3 CFR (1974).

ROUTINE USES OF RECORDS MAINTAINED IN THE SYSTEM, INCLUDING CATEGORIES OF USERS AND THE PURPOSES OF SUCH USES:

Data in NCIC files is exchanged with and for the official use of authorized officials of the Federal Government, the States, cities, penal and other institutions, and certain foreign governments. The data is exchanged through NCIC lines to Federal criminal justice agencies, criminal justice agencies in the 50 States, the District of Columbia, Puerto Rico, U.S. Possessions {PG 49153} and U.S. Territories. Additionally, data contained in the various "want files," i.e., the stolen vehicle file, stolen license plate file, stolen missing gun file, stolen article file, wanted person file, securities file and boat file may be accessed by the Royal Canadian Mounted Police. Criminal history data is disseminated to non-criminal justice agencies for use in connection with licensing for local/state employment or other uses, but only where such dissemination is authorized by Federal or state statutes and approved by the Attorney General of the United States.

Data in NCIC files, other than the Computerized Criminal History File, is disseminated to:

(1) A nongovernmental agency or subunit thereof which allocates a substantial part of its annual budget to the administration of criminal justice, whose regularly employed peace officers have full police powers pursuant to state law and have complied with the minimum employment standards of governmentally employed police officers as specified by state statute;

(2) A noncriminal justice governmental department of motor vehicle or driver's license registry established by a statute, which provides vehicles registration and driver record information to criminal justice agencies;

(3) A governmental regional dispatch center, established by a state statute, resolution, ordinance or Executive order, which provides communications services to criminal justice agencies; and

(4) the national Automobile Theft Bureau, a nongovernmental nonprofit agency which acts as a national clearinghouse for information on stolen vehicles and offers free assistance to law enforcement agencies concerning automobile thefts, identification and recovery of stolen vehicles.

Disclosures of information from this system, as described above, are for the purpose of providing information to authorized agencies to facilitate the apprehension of fugitives, the location of missing persons, the location and/or return of stolen property, or similar criminal justice objectives.

Information on missing children, missing adults who were reported missing while children, and unidentified living and deceased persons may be disclosed to the National Center for Missing and Exploited Children (NCMEC). The NCMEC is a nongovernmental, nonprofit, federally funded corporation, serving as a national resource and technical assistance clearinghouse focusing on missing and exploited children. Information is disclosed to NCMEC to assist it in its efforts to provide technical assistance and education to parents and local governments regarding the problems of missing and exploited children, and to operate a nationwide missing children hotline to permit members of the public to telephone the Center from anywhere in the United States with information about a missing child.

In addition, information may be released to the news media and the public pursuant to 28 CFR 50.2, unless it is determined that release of the specific information in the context of a particular case would constitute an unwarranted invasion of personal privacy;

To a Member of Congress or staff acting upon the member's behalf whom the member or staff requests the information on behalf of and at the request of the individual who is the subject of the record; and, To the National Archives and Records Administration and the General Services Administration in records management inspections conducted under the authority of 44 U.S.C. 2904 and 2906.

POLICIES AND PRACTICES FOR STORING, RETRIEVING, ACCESSING, RETAINING, AND DISPOSING OF RECORDS IN THE SYSTEM:

STORAGE:

Information maintained in the NCIC system is stored electronically for use in a computer environment.

RETRIEVABILITY:

On-line access to data in NCIC is achieved by using the following search descriptors.

1. Vehicle file:
    - (a) Vehicle identification number;
    - (b) License plate number;
    - (c) NCIC number (unique number assigned by the NCIC computer to each NCIC record).
2. License Plate File:
    - (a) License plate number;
    - (b) NCIC number.
3. Gun file:
    - (a) Serial number of gun;
    - (b) NCIC number.

4. Article File:

   (a) Serial number of article;

   (b) NCIC number.

5. Wanted Person File, U.S. Secret Service Protective File, Foreign Fugitive File, and Canadian Warrant File:

   (a) Name and one of the following numerical identifiers, date of birth, FBI Number (number assigned by the Federal Bureau of Investigation to an arrest fingerprint record). Social Security number (it is noted the requirements of the Privacy Act with regard to the solicitation of Social Security numbers have been brought to the attention of the members of the NCIC system). Operator's license number (drivers number). Miscellaneous identifying number (military number or number assigned by Federal, state, or local authorities to an individual's record). Origination agency case number.

   (b) Vehicle or license plate known to be in the possession of the wanted person.

   (c) NCIC number (unique number assigned to each NCIC record).

6. Securities File:

   (a) Type, serial number, denomination of security;

   (b) Type of security and name of owner of security;

   (c) Social Security number of owner of security;

   (d) NCIC number.

7. Boat File:

   (a) Registration document number;

   (b) Hull serial number;

   (c) NCIC number.

8. Computerized Criminal History File:

   (a) Name, sex, race and date of birth;

   (b) FBI number;

   (c) State identification number;

(d) Social Security number;

(e) Miscellaneous number.

9. Missing Person File: Same as "Wanted Person" File, plus the age, sex, race, height and weight, eye and hair color, of the missing individual.

10. Unidentified Person File: Age, sex, race, height and weight, eye and hair color, of the unidentified individual.

SAFEGUARDS:

Data stored in the NCIC is documented criminal justice agency information and access to that data is restricted to duly authorized criminal justice agencies. The following security measures are the minimum to be adopted by all criminal justice agencies having access to the NCIC.

Computerized Criminal History File. These measures are designed to prevent unauthorized access to the system data and/or unauthorized use of data obtained from the computerized file.

1. Computer Center:

   a. The criminal justice agency computer site must have adequate physical security to protect against any unauthorized personnel gaining access to the computer equipment or to any of the stored data.

   b. Since personnel at these computer centers can have access data stored in the system, they must be screened thoroughly under the authority and supervision of an NCIC control terminal agency. (This authority and supervision may be delegated to responsible criminal justice agency personnel in the case of a satellite computer center being serviced through a stated control terminal agency.) This screening will also apply to non-criminal justice maintenance or technical personnel.

   c. All visitors to these computer centers must be accompanied by staff personnel at all times.

   d. Computers having access to the NCIC must have the proper computer instructions written and other built-in controls to prevent criminal history data from being accessible to any terminals other than authorized terminals.

e. Computers having access to the NCIC must maintain a record of all transactions against the criminal history filed in the same manner the NCIC {PG 49154} computer logs all transactions. The NCIC identifies each specific agency entering or receiving information and maintains a record of those transactions. This transaction record must be monitored and reviewed on a regular basis to detect any possible misuse of criminal history data.

f. Each State Control terminal shall build its data system around a central computer, through which each inquiry must pass for screening and verification. The configuration and operation of the center shall provide for the integrity of the data base.

2. Communications:

a. Lines/channels being used to transmit criminal history information must be dedicated solely to criminal justice, i.e., there must be no terminals belonging to agencies outside the criminal justice system sharing these lines/channels.

b. Physical security of the lines/channels must be protected too guard against clandestine devices being utilized to intercept or inject system traffic.

3. Terminal Devices Having Access to NCIC:

a. All agencies having terminals on this system must be required to physically place these terminals in secure locations within the authorized agency.

b. The agencies having terminals with access to criminal history must have terminal operators screened and restricted access to the terminal to a minimum number of authorized employees.

c. Copies of criminal history data obtained from terminal devices must be afforded security to prevent any unauthorized access to or use of the data.

d. All remote terminals on NCIC Computerized Criminal History will maintain a hard copy of computerized criminal history inquiries with notations of individual making request for record (90 days).

RETENTION AND DISPOSAL:

Unless otherwise removed, records will be retained in files as follows:

1. Vehicle File:

   a. Unrecovered stolen vehicle records (including snowmobile records) which do not contain vehicle identification numbers (VIN) therein, will be purged from file 90 days after date of entry.

   b. Unrecovered stolen vehicle records (including snowmobile records) which contain VIN's will remain in file for the year of entry plus 4. Unrecovered vehicles wanted in conjunction with a felony will remain in file for 90 days after entry. In the event a longer retention period is desired, the vehicle must be reentered.

   c. Unrecovered stolen VIN plates, certificates or origin or title, and serially numbered stolen vehicles engines or transmissions will remain in file for the year of entry plus 4. (Job No. NC1-65-82-4, Part E. 13 h.(1))

2. License Plate File:

   Unrecovered stolen license plates not associated with a vehicle will remain in file for one year after the end of the plate's expiration year as shown in the record. (Job No. NC1-65-82- 4, Part E. 13 h.(2))

3. Gun file:

   a. Unrecovered weapons will be retained in file for an indefinite period until action is taken by the originating agency to clear the record.

   b. Weapons entered in file as "recovered" weapons will remain in file for the balance of the year entered plus 2. (Job No. NC1-65-82-4, Part E. 13 h.(3))

4. Article File:

   Unrecovered stolen articles will be retained for the balance of the year entered plus one year. (Job No. NC1-65-82-4, Part E. 13 h.(4))

5. Wanted Person File:

   Person not located will remain in file indefinitely until action is taken by the originating agency to clear the record (except "Temporary Felony Wants", which will be automatically removed from the file after 48 hours). (Job No. NC1-65-87-114, Part E. 13 h.(7))

6. Securities File:

Unrecovered, stolen, embezzled, counterfeited or missing securities will be retained for the balance of the year entered plus 4, except for travelers checks and money orders, which will be retained for the balance of the year entered plus 2. (Job No. NC1-65-82-4, Part E. 13h. (5))

7. Boat File:

Unrecovered stolen boats will be retained in file for the balance of the year entered plus 4. Unrecovered stolen boat records which do not contain a hull serial number will be purged from file 90 days after date of entry. (Job No. NC1-65-82-4, Part E. 13h. (6))

8. Missing Persons File:

Will remain in the file until the individual is located or, in the case of unemancipated persons, the individual reaches the age of emancipation as defined by law of his state. (Job No. N 1-65-87-11, Part E. 13h. (8))

9. Computerized Criminal History File:

When an individual reaches age of 80. (Job No. NC1-65-76-1)

10. U.S. Secret Service Protective File:

Will be retained until names are removed by the U.S. Secret Service.

11. Foreign Fugitive File:

Person not located will remain in file indefinitely until action is taken by the originating agency to clear the record.

12. Canadian Warrant File:

Person and located will remain in file indefinitely until action is taken by the originating agency to clear the record.

13. Unidentified Person File:

Will be retained for the remainder of the year of entry plus 9.

SYSTEM MANAGER(S) AND ADDRESS:

Director, Federal Bureau of Investigation

J. Edgar Hoover Building

10th and Pennsylvania Avenue NW.

Washington, DC 20535

NOTIFICATION PROCEDURE: Same as the above.

RECORD ACCESS PROCEDURE:

It is noted the Attorney General is exempting this system from the access and contest procedures of the Privacy Act. However, the following alternative procedures are available to requester. The procedures by which an individual may obtain a copy of his Computerized Criminal History are as follows:

If an individual has a criminal record supported by fingerprints and that record has been entered in the NCIC CCH File, it is available to that individual for review, upon presentation of appropriate identification and in accordance with applicable State and Federal administrative and statutory regulations.

Appropriate identification includes being fingerprinted for the purpose of insuring that he is the individual that he purports to be. The record on file will then be verified as his through comparison of fingerprints.

PROCEDURE:

1. All requests for review must be made by the subject of his record through a law enforcement agency which has access to the NCIC CCH File. That agency within statutory or regulatory limits can require additional identification to assist in securing a positive identification.

2. If the cooperative law enforcement agency can make an identification with fingerprints previously taken which are on file locally and if the FBI identification number of the individual's record is available to that agency, it can make an on-line inquiry of NCIC to obtain his record on-line or, if it does not have suitable equipment to obtain an on-line response, obtain the record from Washington, DC by mail. The individual will then be afforded the opportunity to see that record.

3. Should the cooperating law enforcement agency not have the individual's fingerprints on file locally, it is necessary for that agency to relate his prints to an existing record by having his identification prints compared with those already on file in the FBI or possibly, in the State's central identification agency.

CONTESTING RECORD PROCEDURES:

The subject of the requested record shall request the appropriate arresting agency, court, or correctional agency to initiate action necessary to correct any stated inaccuracy in his record or provide the information needed to make the record complete.

RECORD SOURCE CATEGORIES:

Information contained in the NCIC system is obtained from local, State, Federal and international criminal justice agencies.

SYSTEMS EXEMPTED FROM CERTAIN PROVISIONS OF THE ACT:

The Attorney General has exempted this system from subsection (c) (3) and (4), (d), (e) (1), (2) and (3), (e)(4) (G), (H), (e)(8) (f) and (g) of the Privacy Act pursuant to 5 U.S.C. 552a (j)(2) and (k)(3). Rules have been promulgated in accordance with the requirements of 5 U.S.C. 553 (b), (c) and (e) and have been published in the Federal Register.

CHAPTER 6

JUSTICE/FBI-002

Federal Bureau of Investigation Central Files System

This system is the granddaddy of them all. It is maintained by and used by the FBI internally. To understand how comprehensive the data is, one must appreciate how sophisticated the FBI is in comparison local police agencies.

Special Agents do not stand around giving out traffic tickets. The Bureau has had to find ways to successfully deal with espionage by the Russian KGB, counter the refined efforts of multi-billion dollar organized crime syndicates, and function efficiently worldwide in many languages and cultures to combat the well-funded high-tech attempts of terrorist organizations and international financial fraudists. And these are just a few of the challenges. They are the best of the best, and not to be ever underestimated in capability.

The central file system is their principle tool . . . the means by which they express the investigative genius which makes the FBI unique. In looking at the detail file description one can readily see the bewildering diversity of areas which constitutes the Bureau's charter. There are 277 different law enforcement areas, each of which is classified and tracked separately.

One can also begin to see how the FBI has gradually gotten out of control over the years. Many of these categories are purely legislative and/or administrative in nature and have very little to do with public dangers. For example, category code 43H "Unauthorized use of the Smokey Bear Symbol", or code 142 "Illegal use of a railroad pass" . . . retirees beware!, or perhaps code 154 "Interstate Transportation of Unsafe Refrigerators", and lets not forget code 180 "Desecration of the Flag".

All humor aside, there are basically three classes of codes in the system. First, of course there are things which no one but an anarchist would question as necessary. Then there are some things which are superfluous and at times humorous as we have just seen. Lastly, there are the classifications which are the signature of a Congress which has gone unchallenged for far too long, an overgrown and overzealous bureaucracy spanning many departments, all of whom empower (unfortunately for the public) an eager and competent FBI.

The tangle of laws, which by now fills a room with volumes, has become far beyond all limits, incomprehensible to the average lawyer, much less a citizen. Many other modern countries get along just fine without this enormous incestuous subculture of "professionals" who interpret (find ways around) laws, which spawn more and increasingly complex laws, which in turn call for more specialists to find ways around them . . . ad nauseum. And all the while, the FBI is busy asking for (and getting) the budget increases to build their empire even larger so that they can "deal with the rapid rise in (contrived non-dangerous) crime".

A QUESTION OF ATTITUDE

The Federal government has always been and continues to be very concerned about "loyalty", especially for positions with overseas service (such as AID, Peace Corps, State Department, etc.) The reason is not particularly apparent until one gets to see first hand, US foreign policy at work. If an official is not very solidly behind Uncle Sam and all it stands for, it would be tempting for him to start basing his actions on objective judgements stemming from real need and obvious realities . . . and that would frequently not be in sync with the official policy.

Of the 277 total categories, at least 18 deal with some aspect of the loyalty issue. For all its considerable armor, the US government is apparently very paranoid. Why? This could be debated forever, but it would not stretch the imagination very far at all to say that privately, it is not particularly proud of its frequently not-well-received foreign policy. But its officials continue to implement policies and directives without question as long as they believe they are "doing what is necessary".

On the domestic side, the condescending nature of "big government" has long since removed the humanity from its public interface. Virtually every government agency is charged with the "duty" of reporting to the FBI any employee who does or says something which brings into question their loyalty (willingness to execute policy). IRS auditors are given productivity quotas to make without any sensitivity to the facts of their cases. The ways to fall victim to the tax laws are uncountable. And the helpless are not exempted. Social Security fraud investigators are given no latitude in prosecuting senior citizens who may have underreported a little income in an attempt to receive their whole benefit and make ends meet . . . which brings us to the next major category of investigations.

As you will read, there is quite a lot discussion concerning "Fraud against the government". At first glimpse, this phrase appears pretty awful and certainly unamerican. But, after you get past some very real and quite brazen criminal fraud, there are thousands of cases of minor infractions by common citizens, many of whom simply got trapped in the "system" . . . and had their lives destroyed. How many people are really certain that they have met every requirement for their Small Business Administration loan or farm subsidy. There is no compassion in the government-citizen interface . . . no way back, once someone "comes to the notice of the government".

FRAUD AGAINST THE GOVERNMENT AND LOYALTY GO TOGETHER

Any official who balks at maintaining an indifferent and "official" demeanor is at risk of having their loyalty questioned. Why? Because the official position has come to be one of condescension. Many, if not most career officials actually believe that, only the government is wise enough to know what is good for the American people . . . that the people are capable of making no judgement at all for themselves. They must be led, controlled, but especially watched, in every aspect of their lives.

So again, we have the paradox of the FBI, guardian of the "American Way" (whatever that is). It is the enforcement arm of a self-serving, misguided, and invasive government and does without questioning, whatever it is told to do. Given the Bureau's resources, and its own attitude which has evolved over the years, this makes them potentially very dangerous. I have been informed by bureau personnel who, speaking in all seriousness, stated that "it would make our job easier if we had a dossier on everyone living in the United States."

THE CENTRAL FILE INDEXES

The sheer volume of data amassed in the Central File system presents a challenge to render it usable. The FBI has therefore established a series of indexes, maintained both at headquarters and at field offices. These indexes, some of which are actual extracted subfiles, are cross-referenced by nature of investigation in the Central File data. The very existence of certain indexes and the way they are organized, reveal a number of interesting things.

The Administrative Index (ADEX) was actively used from 1971 till 1978. (It still exists for reference purposes) It is made up of people who are believed to constitute a potential or active threat to the internal security of the United States . . . in other words, civil rights activists and others who vocally disagree with some aspect of government. That it was used ever, is ample proof that it would be used again should we go into another period of heightened public awareness and criticism.

The Channeling Index consists of names and addresses of people frequently mentioned in informant reports. It facilitates routing to the appropriate file categories. That a special index is needed to handle the volume of informant information, is testimony to size and extent of that FBI activity. Another related index is simply entitled, the Criminal Informant Index, and contains background information on all informants. In addition, there is a separate comprehensive Informant Index maintained at all 56 field offices. Then, there exists in 15 field offices, a extensive cross-reference to the other field offices informant indexes. And finally, there is the Security Informants Index maintained at headquarters. There can be no doubt. Informants are big business at the FBI.

Separate from all this, is the Top Echelon Criminal Informer Program Index (TECIP). This index contains background information on those people who are either furnishing high level information, or are "under development" to do so.

This last phrase is intriguing and confirms that the FBI has a professional informants training program. The use of informants is an insidious aspect of monitoring a society. It undermines the very substance on which trust is built. Trust is a prime ingredient of a successful culture. By removing trust of the public, law enforcement is killing the very essence of crime prevention. The paradox should be obvious.

The Sources of Information Index consists of individuals and organizations such as banks, motels, and local government that are willing to furnish information to the FBI. This particular category of sources is particularly exposed to the practice of "persuasion" to guarantee their continuing cooperation.

The Special Services Index contains names of "prominent" people who are in a position to "furnish assistance" to the FBI. Here's one that's food for thought!

These last several topics mentioned are the key to the element of FBI methods which pose the greatest public danger. The massive use of informants, most of which have been intimidated into being such, constitutes a grave invasion of privacy . . . and inevitably leads to government by fear. This goes well beyond simply looking for real criminals. It instills a bona fide dread of all things government and however unwilling, people begin to give in and report their neighbors for anything and everything, just in the hope of exempting themselves from the wrath of the government. This is a very sure formula to break the spirit of a nation.

The False Identities Index contain names of deceased individuals whose birth certificates have been obtained by other persons. This is obviously a program to stop paper tripping.

Interestingly, this index is no longer updated, (although it remains accessible) apparently in light of progress at the state level at cross-referencing birth and death certificates. There is both a program at headquarters, as well as a program at the field office level. In addition, field offices maintain a photo album of people who have been identified as using alternate identities.

Not surprisingly, there is a Fraud Against the Government Index. It is maintained at the field office level.

The Leased Line Letter Request Index contains information regarding letters to the telephone company requesting leased lines for wire taps. This is an insight into operating procedures. Gone are the days of an agent up on a telephone pole or crouched furtively in the basement of an apartment building. The desired number to be monitored is simply switched to a central location by way of a leased line.

Also, if the Bureau chooses to use it, the technology exists to monitor a line or group of lines automatically. By use of a specialized computer, it can even automatically scan many conversations at once for "key words", then turn on continuous recording for those who fail their "filter."

The Mail Cover Index is a record of all mail cover requests since 1973. To understand the significance of this it is necessary to define "mail cover". Simply stated, it is the ability of the FBI to demand that a local postmaster inspect a subject's mail and intercept all or certain kinds. I will leave the implications of this to your imagination.

The Prostitute Photo Album contains data on anyone who has been arrested for prostitution by any authority in the United States. Ostensibly to aid in investigations under the White Slave Traffic Act, these files could haunt many a young girl for the rest of their lives.

The Toll Record Request Index, and Telephone Subscriber and Toll Records Check Index both relate to requests made to the phone companies for histories of numbers called. This is a very commonly used practice for developing information on a citizen both before and after he is charged with a crime.

The Veterans Administration (VA)/Federal Housing Administration (FHA) Matters Index is described very ambiguously. Kept at the field office level, it is simply stated that it contains individuals who are the subject of VA or FHA investigation. Both of these agencies handle home mortgages, and one can only imagine what happens to the personal information given out on the application forms.

The remainder of the indexs are conventional criminal files. The are cleverly conceived and give a good idea of how the Bureau operates.

SECURITY

The safeguards which have been put into place for the various elements of the Central Files system are comparable with military measures. This includes use of encrypted data and phone links, Armed Forces courier services, and of course, serious physical security. No access whatsoever is permitted to other than FBI employees. Any approved requests for FBI data (from other police agencies, etc.) are filled inside of secure FBI office space by FBI employees.

POLICIES AND PROCEDURES

The majority of the Central Files has been exempted from the Privacy Act in such a way that, though an individual may request access or correct his file, the FBI reserves the right to refuse that request. Further to that, it has been established that the Bureau often investigates, or as a minimum starts a file on, anyone who contacts them for information. The routine uses of the system go on for pages. Suffice to say that it is all official and can be used in any way to further the objectives of the FBI.

At the end of the description of this system is a list of field office and legal attaché locations. The FBI is well represented with 57 offices in the US plus 6 European countries, 5 Latin American countries, Canada, Japan, Australia, Philippines, and Hong Kong. The attachés are located in the respective embassies. Note well these locations if you have any concerns about needing to visit your embassy abroad. Also be assured that these offices have ready access to the computer files

GOVERMENT TEXT

JUSTICE/FBI-002

SYSTEM NAME: The FBI Central Records System

SYSTEM LOCATIONS:

A. Federal Bureau of Investigation,
J. Edgar Hoover Building,
10th and Pennsylvania Avenue, NW.,
Washington, DC 20535;

B. 56 field divisions (see Appendix);

C. 16 Legal Attachés (see Appendix).

CATEGORIES OF INDIVIDUALS COVERED BY THE SYSTEM:

A) Individuals who relate in any manner to official FBI investigations including, but not limited to subjects, suspects, victims, witnesses, and close relatives and associates who are relevant to an investigation.

B) Applicants for and current and former personnel of the FBI and persons related thereto who are considered relevant to an applicant investigation, personnel inquiry, or other personnel matters.

C) Applicants for and appointees to sensitive positions in the United States Government and persons related thereto who are considered relevant to the investigation.

D) Individuals who are the subject of unsolicited information, who offer unsolicited information, request assistance, and make inquiries concerning record material, including general correspondence, and contacts with other agencies, businesses, institutions, clubs; the public and the news media.

E) Individuals associated with administrative operations or services including pertinent functions, contractors and pertinent persons related thereto.

(All manner of information concerning individuals may be acquired in connection with and relating to the varied investigative responsibilities of the FBI which are further described in

"CATEGORIES OF RECORDS IN THE SYSTEM." Depending on the nature and scope of the investigation this information may include, among other things, personal habits and conduct, financial information, travel and organizational affiliation of individuals. The information collected is made a matter of record and placed in FBI files).

CATEGORIES OF RECORDS IN THE SYSTEM

The FBI Central Records Systems – The FBI utilizes a central records system of maintaining its investigative, personnel, applicant, administrative, and general files. This system consists of one numerical sequence of subject matter files, an alphabetical index to the files, and a supporting abstract system to facilitate processing and accountability of all important mail placed in files. This abstract system is both a textual and an automated capability for locating mail. Files kept in FBI field offices are also structured in the same manner, except they do not utilize an abstract system.

The FBI uses 277 classifications in its basic filing system which pertain primarily to Federal violations over which the FBI has investigative jurisdiction. However, included in the 277 classifications are personnel, applicant, and administrative matters to facilitate the overall filing scheme. These classifications are as follows (the word "obsolete" following the name of the classification indicates the FBI is no longer initiating investigative cases in these matters, although the material is retained for reference purposes):

1. Training Schools; National Academy Matters: FBI National Academy Applicants. Covers general information concerning the FBI National Academy, including background investigations of individual candidates.
2. Neutrality Matters. Title 18, United States Code, Sections 956 and 958 962; Title 22, United States Code, Sections 1934 and 401.
3. Overthrow or Destruction of the Government. Title 18, United States Code, Section 2385.
4. National Firearms Act, Federal Firearms Act; State Firearms Control Assistance Act; Unlawful Possession or Receipt of Firearms. Title 26, United States Code, Sections 5801-5812; Title 18, United States Code, Sections 921-928; Title 18, United States Code. Sections 1201-1203.

5. Income Tax. Covers violations of Federal income tax laws reported to the FBI. Complaints are forwarded to the Commissioner of the Internal Revenue Service.

6. Interstate Transportation of Strikebreakers. Title 18, United States Code, Section 1231.

7. Kidnapping. Title 28, United States Code, Sections 1201 and 1202.

8. Migratory Bird Act. Title 18, United States Code, Section 43; Title 16, United States Code, Section 703 through 718.

9. Extortion. Title 18, United States Code Sections 876, 877, 875, and 873.

10. Red Cross Act. Title 18, United States Code, Sections 706 and 917.

11. Tax (Other than Income) This classification covers complaints concerning violations of Internal Revenue law as they apply to other than alcohol, social security and income and profits taxes, which are forwarded to the Internal Revenue Service.

12. Narcotics. This classification covers complaints received by the FBI concerning alleged violations of Federal drug laws. Complaints are forwarded to the headquarters of the Drug Enforcement Administration (DEA), or the nearest district office of DEA.

13. Miscellaneous. Section 125, National Defense Act, Prostitution; Selling Whiskey Within Five Miles of An Army Camp. 1920 only. Subjects were alleged violators of abuse of U.S. flag, fraudulent enlistment, selling liquor and operating houses of prostitution within restricted bounds of military reservations. Violations of Section 13 of the Selective Service Act (Conscription Act were enforced by the Department of Justice as a war emergency measure with the Bureau exercising jurisdiction in the detection and prosecution of cases within the purview of that Section.

14. Sedition. Title 18, United States Code, Sections 2387, 2388, and 2391.

15. Theft from Interest Shipment. Title 18, United States Code, Section 859; Title 18, United States Code, Section 660; Title 18 United States Code, Section 2117.

16. Violations of Federal Injunction (obsolete). Consolidated into Classification 69, "Contempt of Court".

17. Fraud Against the Government Department of Veterans Affairs, Department of Veterans Affairs Matters. Title 18, United States Code, Section 287, 289, 290, 371, or 1001, and Title 38, United States Code, Sections 787(a), 787(b), 3405, 3501, and 3502.

18. May Act. Title 18, United States Code, Section 1384. {PG 49156}

19. Censorship Matter (obsolete). Pub. L. 77th Congress.

20. Federal Grain Standards Act (obsolete) 1920 only. Subjects were alleged violators of contracts for sale. Shipment of Interstate Commerce, Section 5, U.S. Grain Standards Act.

21. Food and Drugs. This classification covers complaints received concerning alleged violations of the Food, Drug and Cosmetic Act; Tea Act; Import Milk Act; Caustic Poison Act; and Filled Milk Act. These complaints are referred to the Commissioner of the Food and Drug Administration of the field component of that Agency.

22. National Motor Vehicle Traffic Act, 1922-27 (obsolete). Subjects were possible violators of the National Motor Vehicle Theft Act, Automobiles seized by Prohibitions Agents.

23. Prohibition. This classification covers complaints received concerning bootlegging activities and other violations of the alcohol tax laws. Such complaints are referred to the Bureau of Alcohol, Tobacco and Firearms, Department of the Treasury, or field representatives of the Agency.

24. Profiteering 1920-42. (obsolete). Subject are possible violators of the Lever Act-Profiteering in food and clothing or accused company was subject of file. Bureau conducted investigations to ascertain profits.

25. Selective Service Act; Selective Training and Service Act. Title 50, United States Code, Section 462; Title 50 United States Code, Section 459.

26. Interstate Transportation of Stolen Motor Vehicle; Interstate Transportation of Stolen Aircraft. Title 18, United States Code, Sections 2311 (in part), 2312, and 2313.

27. Patent Matter. Title 35, United States Code, Sections 104 and 105.

28. Copyright Matter. Title 17, United States Code, Sections 104 and 105.

29. Bank Fraud and Embezzlement. Title 18, United States Code, Sections 212, 213, 215, 334, 655-657, 1004-1006, 1008, 1009, 1014, and 1306; Title 12, United States Code, Section 1725(g).

30. Interstate Quarantine Law, 1922-25 (obsolete). Subjects alleged violators of Act of February 15, 1893, as amended, regarding interstate travel of persons afflicted with infectious diseases. Cases also involved unlawful transportation of animals, Act of February 2, 1903. Referrals were made to Public Health Service and the Department of Agriculture.

31. White Slave Traffic Act. Title 18, United States Code, Section 2421-2424.

32. Identification (Fingerprint) Matters. This classification covers general information concerning Identification (fingerprint) matters.

33. Uniform Crime Reporting. This classification covers general information concerning the Uniform Crime Reports, a periodic compilation of statistics of criminal violations throughout the United States.

34. Violation of Lacy Act. 1922-43. (obsolete) Unlawful Transportation and shipment of black bass and fur seal skins.

35. Civil Service. This classification covers complaints received by the FBI concerning Civil Service matters which are referred to the Office of Personnel Management in Washington or regional offices of that Agency.

36. Mail Fraud. Title 18, United States Code, Section 13341.

37. False Claims Against the Government. 1921-22. (obsolete) Subjects submitted claims for allotment, vocational training, compensation as veterans under the Sweet Bill. Letters were generally referred elsewhere (Veterans Bureau). Violators apprehended for violation of Article No. 1, War Risk Insurance Act.

38. Application for Pardon to Restore Civil Rights.
1921-35. (obsolete) Subjects allegedly obtained their naturalization papers by fraudulent means. Cases later referred to Immigration and Naturalization Service.

39. Falsely Claiming Citizenship. (obsolete) Title 18, United States Code, Sections 911 and 1015(a)(b).

40. Passport and Visa Matter. Title 18, United States Code, Sections 1451-1546.

41. Explosives (obsolete). Title 50, United States Code, Sections 121 through 144.

42. Deserter; Deserter, Harboring. Title 10, United States Code, Sections 808 and 885.

43. Illegal Wearing of Uniforms; False Advertising or Misuse of Names, Words, Emblems or Insignia;

* Illegal Manufacturer, Use, Possession, or Sale of Emblems and Insignia;
* Illegal Manufacture, Possession, or Wearing of Civil Defense Insignia;
* Miscellaneous, Forging or Using Forged Certificate of Discharge from Military or Naval Service;
* Miscellaneous, Falsely Making or Forging Naval, Military, or Official Pass;
* Miscellaneous, Forging or Counterfeiting Seal of Department or Agency of the United States,

* Misuse of the Great Seal of the United States or of the Seals of the President or the Vice President of the United States;
* Unauthorized Use of "Johnny Horizon" Symbol;
* Unauthorized Use of Smokey Bear Symbol.
* Title 18, United States Code, Sections 702, 703, and 704;
* Title 18, United States Code, Sections 701, 705, 707, and 710;
* Title 36, United States Code, Section 182;
* Title 50, Appendix, United States Code, Section 2284;
* Title 46, United States Code, Section 249;
* Title 18, United States Code, Sections 498, 499, 506, 709, 711, 711a, 712, 713, and 714;
* Title 12, United States Code, Sections 1457 and 1723a;
* Title 22, United States Code, Section 2518.

44. Civil Rights; Civil Rights, Election Laws, Voting Rights Act, 1965, Title 18, United States Code, Sections 241, 242, and 245; Title 42, United States Code, Section 1973; Title 18, United States Code, Section 243; Title 18, United States Code, Section 244, Civil Rights Act-Federally Protected Activities; Civil Rights Act-Overseas Citizens Voting Rights Act of 1975.

45. Crime on the High Seas (Includes stowaways on boats and aircraft). Title 18, United States Code, Sections 7, 13, 1243, and 2199.

46. Fraud Against the Government: (Includes:
* Department of Health, Education and Welfare;
* Department of Labor (CETA), and
* Miscellaneous Government Agencies)
* Anti-Kickback Statute; Department Assistance Act of 1950;
* False Claims, Civil; Federal-Aid Road Act;
* Lead and Zinc Act; Public Works and Economic Development Act of 1965;
* Renegotiation Act, Criminal;
* Renegotiation Act, Civil;
* Trade Expansion Act of 1962;
* Unemployment Compensation Statutes;
* Economic Opportunity Act.
* Title 50, United States Code, Section 1211 et seq.;
* Title 31, United States Code, Section 231;
* Title 41, United States Code, Section 119;
* Title 40, United States Code, Section 489.

47. Impersonation. Title 18, United States Code, Section 912, 913, 915, and 916.

48. Postal Violation (Except Mail Fraud). This classification covers inquiries concerning the Postal Service and complaints pertaining to the theft of mail. Such complaints are either forwarded to the Postmaster General or the nearest Postal Inspector.

49. Bankruptcy Fraud. Title 18, United States Code, Sections 151-155.

50. Involuntary Servitude and Slavery. U.S. Constitution, 13th Amendment; Title 18, United States Code, sections 1581-1588, 241, and 242.

51. Jury Panel Investigations. This classification covers jury panel investigations which are requested by the appropriate Assistant Attorney General as authorized by 28 U.S.C. 533 and AG memorandum 781, dated 11/9/72. These investigations can be conducted only upon such a request and consist of an indices and arrest check, and only in limited important trials where defendant could have influence over a juror. {PG 49157}

52. Theft, Robbery, Embezzlement, Illegal Possession or Destruction of Government Property. Title 18, United States Code, Sections 641, 1024, 1660, 2112, and 2114. Interference With Government Communications, Title 18, U.S.C., Section 1632.

53. Excess Profits On Wool. 1918 (obsolete). Subjects possible violator of Government Control of Wool Clip of 1918.

54. Customs Laws and Smuggling. This classification covers complaints received concerning smuggling and other matters involving importation and entry of merchandise into and the exportation of merchandise from the United States. Complaints are referred to the nearest district office of the U.S. Customs Service or the Commissioner of Customs, Washington, DC.

55. Counterfeiting. This classification covers complaints received concerning alleged violations of counterfeiting of U.S. coins, notes, and other obligations and securities of the Government. These complaints are referred to either the Director, U.S. Secret Service, or the nearest office of that Agency.

56. Election Laws. Title 18, United States Code, Sections 241, 242, 245, and 591-607; Title 42, United States Code, Section 1973; Title 26, United States Code, Sections 9012 and 9042; Title 2, United States Code, Sections 431-437, 439, and 441.

57. War Labor Dispute Act (obsolete). Pub. L. 89-77th Congress.

58. Corruption of Federal Public Officials. Title 18, United States Code, Sections 201-203, 205-211; Pub. L. 89-4 and 89-136.

59. World War Adjusted Compensation Act of 1924-44. (obsolete) Bureau of Investigation was charged with the duty of investigating alleged violations of all sections of the World War Adjusted Compensation Act (Pub. L. 472, 69th Congress (H.R. 10277)) with the exception of Section 704.

60. Anti-Trust, Title 15, United States Code, Sections 1-7, 12-27, and 13.

61. Treason or Misprision of Treason. Title 18, United States Code, Sections 2381, 2382, 2389, 2390, 756, and 757.

62. Administrative Inquiries.
    * Misconduct Investigations of Officers and Employees of the Department of Justice and Federal Judiciary;
    * Census Matters (Title 13, United States Code, Sections 211- 214, 221-224, 304, and 305)
    * Domestic Police Cooperation;
    * Eight-Hour-Day Law (Title 40, United States Code, Sections 321, 332, 325a, 326);
    * Fair Credit Reporting Act (Title 15, United States Code, Sections 1681q and 1681r);
    * Federal Cigarette Labeling and Advertising Act (Title 15, United States Code, Section 1333);
    * Federal Judiciary Investigations;
    * Kickback Racket Act (Title 18, United States Code, Section 874);
    * Lands Division Matter, other Violations and/or Matters;
    * Civil Suits – Miscellaneous;
    * Soldiers' and Sailors' Civil Relief Act of 1940 (Title 50, Appendix, United States Code, Sections 510-590);
    * Tariff Act of 1930 (Title 19, United States Code, Section 1304),
    * Unreported Interstate Shipment of Cigarettes (Title 15, United States Code, Sections 375 and 376);
    * Fair Labor Standards Act of 1938 (Wages and Hours Law) (Title 29, United States Code, Sections 201-219);
    * Conspiracy (Title 18, United States Code, Section 371 (formerly Section 88, Title 18, United States Code); effective September 1, 1948).

63. Miscellaneous – Nonsubversive. This classification concerns correspondence from the public which does not relate to matters within FBI jurisdiction.

64. Foreign Miscellaneous. This classification is a control file utilized as a repository for intelligence information of value identified by country. More specific categories are placed in classification 108-113.

65. Espionage. Attorney General Guidelines on Foreign Counterintelligence; Internal Security Act of 1950; Executive Order 11905.

66. Administrative Matters. This classification covers such items as supplies, automobiles, salary matters and vouchers.

67. Personnel Matters. This classification concerns background investigations of applicants for employment with the FBI and folders for current and former employees.

68. Alaskan matters (obsolete). This classification concerns FBI investigations in the Territory of Alaska prior to its becomming a State.

69. Contenpt of Court. Title 18, United States Code, Sections 401, 402, 3285, 3691,3692; Title 10, United States Code. Section 847; and Rule 42, Federal Rules of Criminal Procedure.

70. Crime on Government Reservation. Title 18, United States Code, Sections 7 and 13.

71. Bills of Lading Act, Title 49, United States Code, Section 121.

72. Obstruction of Criminal Investigations: Obstruction of Justice, Obstruction of Court Orders. Title 18, United States Code. Sections 1503 through 1510.

73. Application for Pardon After Completion of Sentence and Application for Executive Clemency. This classification concerns the FBI's background investigation in connection with pardon applications and request for executive clemency.

74. Perjury. Title 18, United States Code, Sections 1621, 1622, and 1623.

75. Bondsmen and Sureties. Title 18, United States Code, Section 1506.

76. Escaped Federal Prisoner. Escape and Rescue; Probation Violator, Parole Violator Parole Violator, Mandatory Release Violator. Title 18, United State Code, Sections 751-757, 1072; Title 18. United States Code. Sections 3651-3656; and Title 18, United States Code. Sections 4202-4207, 5037, and 4161-4166.

77. Applicants (Special Inquiry, Departmental and Other Government Agencies, except those having special classifications). This classification covers the background investigations conducted by the FBI in connection with the aforementioned positions.

78. Illegal Use of Government Transportation Requests. Title 18, United States Code, Section 287, 495, 508, 641, 1001 and 1002.

79. Missing Persons. This classification covers the FBI's Identification Division's assistance in the locating of missing persons.

80. Laboratory Research Matters. At FBI Headquarters this classification is used for Laboratory research matters. In field office files this classification covers the FBI's public affairs matters and involves contact by the FBI with the general public, Federal and State agencies, the Armed Forces, Corporations, the news media and other outside organizations.

81. Gold Hoarding. 1933-45. (obsolete) Gold Hoarding investigations conducted in accordance with an Act of March 9, 1933 and Executive Order issued August 28, 1933. Bureau instructed by Department to conduct no further investigations in 1935 under the Gold Reserve Act of 1934. Thereafter, all correspondence referred to Secret Service

82. War Risk Insurance (National Life Insurance (obsolete)). This classification covers investigations conducted by the FBI in connection with civil suits filed under this statute.

83. Court of Claims. This classification covers requests for investigations of cases pending in the Bourt of Claims from the Assistant Attorney General in charge of the Civil Division of the Department of Justice.

84. Reconstruction Finance Corporation Act (obsolete). Title 15, United States Code, Chapter 14.

85. Home Owner Loan Corporation (obsolete). This classification concerned complaints received by the FBI about alleged violations of the Home Owners Loan Act, which were referred to the Home Owners Loan Corporation. Title 12 United States Code, Section 1464. {PG 49158}

86. Fraud Against the Government – Small Business Administration. Title 15, United States Code, Section 645; Title 18, United States Code, Sections 212, 213, 215, 216, 217, 657, 658, 1006, 1011, 1013, 1014, 1906, 1907, and 1909.

87. Interstate Transportation of Stolen Property (Heavy Equipment – Commercialized Theft). Title 18, United States Code, Sections 2311, 2314, 2315 and 2318.

88. Unlawful Flight to Avoid Prosecution, Custody, or Confinement; Unlawful Flight to Avoid Giving Testimony. Title 18, United States Code, Sections 1073 and 1074.

89. Assaulting or Killing a Federal Officer, Crimes Against Family Members, Congressional Assassination Statute, Title 18, United States Code, Sections 1111, 1114, 2232.

90. Irregularities in Federal Penal Institutions. Title 18, United States Code, Sections 1791 and 1792.

91. Bank Burglary; Bank Larcency; Bank Robbery. Title 18, United States Code, Section 2113.

92. Racketeer Enterprise Investigations. Title 18, United States Code. Section 3237.

93. Ascertaining Financial Ability. This classification concerns requests by the Department of Justice for the FBI to ascertain a person's ability to pay a claim, fine or judgment obtained against him by the United States Government.

94. Research matters. This classification concerns all general correspondence of the FBI with private individuals which does not involve any substantive violation of Federal law.

95. Laboratory Cases (Examination of Evidence in Other Than Bureau's Cases). The classification concerns non-FBI cases where a duly constituted State, county or a municipal law enforcement agency in a criminal matter has requested an examination of evidence by the FBI Laboratory.

96. Alien Applicant (obsolete). Title 10, United States Code, Section 310.

97. Foreign Agents Registration Act. Title 18, United States Code, Section 951; Title 22, United States Code, Sections 611-621; Title 50, United States Code, Sections 851-857.

98. Sabotage. Title 18, United States Code, Sections 2151-2156; Title 50, United States Code, Section 797.

99. Plant Survey (obsolete). This classification covers a program wherein the FBI inspected industrial plants for the purpose of making suggestions to the operations of those plants to prevent espionage and sabotage.

100. Domestic Security. This classification covers investigations by the FBI in the domesitc security field, e.g., Smith Act violations.

101. Hatch Act (obsolete). Pub. L. 252, 76th Congress.

102. Voorhis Act, Title 18, United States Code, Section 1386.

103. Interstate Transportation of Stolen Livestock, Title 18, United States Code, Sections 667, 2311, 2316 and 2317.

104. Servicemen's Dependents Allowance Act of 1942 (obsolete). Pub. L 625, 77th Congress, Sections 115-119.

105. Foreign Counterintelligence Matters. Attorney General Guidelines on Foreign Counterintelligence. Executive Order 11905.

106. Alien Enemy Control; Escaped Prisoners of War and Internees, 1944-55 (obsolete). Suspects were generally suspected escaped prisoners of war, members of foreign

organizations, failed to register under the Alien Registration Act. Cases ordered closed by Attorney General after alien enemies returned to their respective countries upon termination of hostilities.

107. Denaturalization Proceedings (obsolete). This classification covers investigations concerning allegations that an individual fraudulently swore allegiance to the United States or in some other manner illegally obtained citizenship to the U.S., Title 8, United States Code, Section 738.

108. Foreign Travel Control (obsolete). This classification concerns security-type investigations wherein the subject is involved in foreign travel.

109. Foreign Political Matters. This classification is a control file utilized as a repository for intelligence information concerning foreign political matters broken down by country.

110. Foreign Economic Matters. This classification is a control file utilized as a repository for intelligence information concerning foreign economic matters broken down by country.

111. Foreign Social Conditions. This classification is a control file utilized as a repository for intelligence information concerning foreign social conditions broken down by country.

112. Foreign Funds. This classification is a control file utilized as a repository for intelligence information concerning foreign funds broken down by country.

113. Foreign Military and Naval Matters. This classification is a control file utilized as a repository for intelligence information concerning foreign military and naval matters broken down by country.

114. Alien Property Custodian Matter (obsolute). Title 50, United States Code, Sections 1 through 38. This classification covers investigations concerning ownership and control of property subject to claims and litigation under this statute.

115. Bond Default; Bail Jumper. Title 18, United States Code, Sections 3146-3152.

116. Department of Energy Applicant; Department of Energy, Employee. This classification concerns background investigations conducted in connection with employment with the Department of Energy.

117. Department of Energy, Criminal. Title 42, United States Code, Sections 2011-2281; Pub. L. 93- 438.

118. Applicant, Intelligence Agency (obsolete). This classification covers applicant background investigations conducted of persons under consideration for employment by the Central Intelligence Group.

119. Federal Regulation of Lobbying Act. Title 2, United States Code, Sections 261-270.

120. Federal Tort Claims Act, Title 28, United States Code, Sections 2671 to 2680. Investigations are conducted pursuant to specific request from the Department of Justice in connection with cases in which the Department of Justice represents agencies sued under the Act.

121. Loyalty of Government Employees (obsolute). Executive Order 9835.

122. Labor Management Relations Act, 1947. Title 29, United States Code, Sections 161, 162, 176-178 and 186.

123. Section Inquiry, States Department, Voice of America (U.S. Information Center) (Pub. L. 402, 80th Congress) (obsolute). This classification covers loyalty and security investigations on personnel employed by or under consideration for employment for Voice of America.

124. European Recovery Program Administration, formerly Foreign Operations Administration, Economic Cooperation Administration or E.R.P., European Recovery Programs; A.I.D., Agency for International Development (obsolete). This classification covers security and loyalty investigations of personnel employed by or under consideration for employment with the European Recovery Program. Pub. L. 472, 80th Congress.

125. Railway Labor Act; Railway Labor Act-Employer's Liability Act Title 45, United States Code, Sections 151-163 and 181-188.

126. National Security Resources Board, Special Inquiry (obsolete). This classification covers loyalty investigations on employees and applicants of the National Security Resources Board.

127. Sensitive Positions in the United States Government, Pub. L. 266 (obsolete). Pub. L. 81st Congress. {PG 49159}

128. International Development Program (Foreign Operations Administration) (obsolete). This classification covers background investigations conducted on individuals who are to be assigned to duties under the International Development Program.

129. Evacuation Claims (obsolete). Pub. L. 886, 80th Congress.

130. Special Inquiry. Armed Forces Security Act (obsolete). This classification covers applicant-type investigations conducted for the Armed Forces security agencies.

131. Admiralty Matter. Title 46, United States Code, Sections 741-752 and 781-799.

132. Special Inquiry, Office of Defense Mobilization (obsolete). This classification covers applicant-type investigations of individuals associated with the Office of Defense Mobilization.

133. National Science Foundation Act, Applicant (obsolete). Pub. L. 507, 81st Congress.

134. Foreign Counterintelligence Assets. This classification concerns individuals who provide information to the FBI concerning Foreign Counterintelligence matters.

135. PROSAB (Protection of Strategic Air Command Bases of the U.S. Air Force (obsolete). This classification covered contacts with individuals with the aim to develop information useful to protect bases of the Strategic Air Command.

136. American Legion Contact (obsolete). This classification covered liaison contracts with American Legion offices.

137. Informants. Other than Foreign Counterintelligence Assets. This classification concerns individuals who furnish information to the FBI concerning criminal violations on a continuing and confidential basis.

138. Loyalty of Employees of the United Nations and Other Public International Organizations. This classification concerns FBI investigations based on referrals from the Office of Personnel Management wherein a question or allegation has been received regarding the applicant's loyalty to the U.S. Government as described in Executive Order 10422.

139. Interception of Communications (Formerly, Unauthorized Publication or Use of Communications). Title 47, United States Code, Section 605; Title 47, United States Code, Section 501; Title 18, United States Code, Sections 2510-2513.

140. Security of Government Employees; Fraud Against the Government, Executive Order 10450.

141. False Entries in Records of Interstate Carriers. Title 47, United States Code, Section 220; Title 49, United States Code, Section 20.

142. Illegal Use of Railroad Pass. Title 49, United States Code, Section 1.

143. Interstate Transport of Gambling Devices. Title 15, United States Code, Sections 1171 through 1180.

144. Interstate Transportation of Lottery Tickets. Title 18, United States Code, Section 1301.

145. Interstate Transportation of Obscene Materials. Title 18, United States Code, Sections 1462, 1464 and 1465.

146. Interstate Transporation of Prison-Made Goods. Title 18, United States Code, Sections 1761 and 1762.

147. Fraud Against the Government – Department of Housing and Urban Development, Matters. Title 18, United States Code, Sections 657, 709, 1006, and 1010; Title 12, United States Code, Sections 1709 and 1715.

148. Interstate Transportation of Fireworks. Title 18, United States Code, Section 836.

149. Destruction of Aircraft or Motor Vehicles. Title 18, United States Code, Sections 31-35.

150. Harboring of Federal Fugitives, Statistics (obsolete).

151. (Referral cases received from the Office of Personnel Management under Pub. L. 298). Agency for International Development; Department of Energy; National Aeronautics and Space Administration; Nation Science Foundation; Peace Corps; Action; U.S. Arms Control and Disarmament Agency; World Health Organization; International Labor Organization; International Communications Agency. This classification covers referrrals from the Office of Personnel Management where an allegation has been received regarding an applicant's loyalty to the U.S Government. These referrals refer to applicants from Peace Corps; Department of Energy, National Aeronautics and Space Administration, Nuclear Regulatory Commission, United States Arms Control and Disarmament Agency and the International Communications Agency.

152. Switchblade Knife Act. Title 15, United States Code, Sections 1241- 1244.

153. Automobile Information Disclosure Act. Title 15, United States Code. Sections 1231-1233.

154. Interstate Transportation of Unsafe Refrigerators. Title 15, United States Code, Sections 1211- 1214.

155. National Aeronautics and Space Act of 1958. Title 18, United States Code, Section 799.

156. Employee Retirement Income Security Act. Title 29, United States Code, Sections 1021-1029, 1111, 1131, and 1141; Title 18, United States Code, Sections 644, 1027, and 1954.

157. Civil Unrest. This classification concerns FBI responsibility for reporting information on civil disturbances or demonstrations. The FBI's investigative

responsiblity is based on the Attorney General's Guidelines for Reporting on Civil Disorders and Demonstrations Involving a Federal Interest which became effective April 5, 1976.

158. Labor-Management Reporting and Disclosure Act of 1959 (Security Matter) (obsolete). Pub. L. 86-257, Section 504.

159. Labor-Management Reporting and Disclosure Act of 1959 (Investigative Matter). Title 29, United States Code, Sections 501, 504, 522, and 530.

160. Federal Train Wreck Statute. Title 18. United States Code, Section 1992.

161. Special Inquiries for White House, Congressional Committee and Other Government Agencies. This classification covers investigations requested by the White House. Congressional committees or other Government agencies.

162. Interstate Gambling Activities. This classification covers information acquired concerning the nature and scope of illegal gambling activities in each field office.

163. Foreign Police Cooperation. This classification covers requests by foreign police for the FBI to render investigative assistance to such agencies.

164. Crime Aboard Aircraft. Title 49, United States Code, Sections 1472 and 1473.

165. Interstate Transmission of Wagering Information. Title 18, United States Code, Section 1065.

166. Interstate Transportation in Aid of Racketeering. Title 18, United States Code, Section 1952.

167. Destruction of Interstate Property. Title 15, United States Code, Sections 1281 and 1282.

168. Interstate Transportation of Wagering Paraphernalia. Title 18, United States Code, Section 1953.

169. Hydraulic Brake Fluid Act (obsolete); 76 Stat. 437, Pub. L. 87-637.

170. Extremist Informants (obsolete). This classification concerns individuals who provided information on a continuing basis on various extremist elements.

171. Motor Vehicle Seat Belt Act (obsolete). Pub. L. 88- 201, 80th Congress.

172. Sports Bribery. Title 18, United States Code, Section 244.

173. Public Accommodations. Civil Rights Act of 1964 Public Facilities; Civil Rights Act of 1964 Public Education; {PG 49160} Civil Rights Act of 1964 Employment;

Civil Rights Act of 1964. Title 42, United States Code, Section 2000; Title 18, United States Code. Section 245.

174. Explosives and Incendiary Devices; Bomb Threats (Formerly Bombing Matters; Bombing Matters, Threats). Title 18, United States Code, Section 844.

175. Assaulting, Kidnapping or Killing the President (or Vice President) of the United States. Title 18, United States Code, Section 1751.

176. Anti-riot Laws. Title 18, United States Code, Section 245.

177. Discrimination in Housing. Title 42, United States Code, Sections 3601-3619 and 3631.

178. Interstate Obscene or Harassing Telephone Calls. Title 47, United States Code, Section 223.

179. Extortionate Credit Transactions. Title 18, United States Code, Section 891- 896.

180. Desecration of the Flag. Title 18, United States Code, Section 700.

181. Consumer Credit Protection Act. Title 15, United States Code, Section 1611.

182. Illegal Gambling Business: Illegal Gambling Business, Obstruction; Illegal Gamling Business Forfeiture. Title 18, United States Code, Section 1955; Title 18, United States Code, Section 1511.

183. Racketeer Influence and Corrupt Organizations. Title 18, United States Code, Sections 1961- 1968.

184. Police Killings. This classification concerns investigations conducted by the FBI upon written request from local Chief of Police or duty constituted head of the local agency to actively participate in the investigation of the killing of a police officer. These investigations are based on a Presidential Directive dated June 3, 1971.

185. Protection of Foreign Officials and Officials Guests of the United States. Title 18, United States Code, Sections 112, 970, 1116, 1117 and 1201.

186. Real Eastate Settlement Procedures Act of 1974. Title 12, United States Code, Section 2602; Title 12, United States Code, Section 2606, and Title 12, United States Code, Section 2607.

187. Privacy Act of 1974, Criminal. Title 5, United States Code, Section 552a.

188. Crime Resistance. This classification covers FBI efforts to develop new or improved approaches, techniques, systems, equipment and devices to improve and strengthen law enforcement as mandated by the Omnibus Crime Control and Safe Streets Action of 1968.

189. Equal Credit Opportunity Act. Title 15, United States Code, Section 1691.

190. Freedom of Information/Privacy Acts. This classification covers the creation of a correspondence file to preserve and maintain accurate records concerning the handling of requests for records submitted pursuant to the Freedom of Information-Privacy Acts.

191. False Identity Matters. (obsolete) This classification covers the FBI's study and examination of criminal elements' efforts to create false identities.

192. Hobbs Act-Financial Institutions; Commercial Institutions; Armored Carrier. Title 18, United States Code, Section 1951.

193. Hobbs Act-Commercial Institutions (obsolete). Title 18, United States Code, Section 1951; Title 47, United States Code, Section 506.

194. Hobbs Act-Corruption of Public Officials. Title 18, United States Code, Section 1951.

195. Hobbs Act-Labor Related. Title 18, United States Code, Section 1951.

196. Fraud by Wire. Title 18, United States Code, Section 1343.

197. Civil Actions or Claims Against the Government. This classification covers all civil suits involving FBI matters and most administrative claims filed under the Federal Tort Claims Act arising from FBI activities.

198. Crime on Indian Reservations. Title 18, United States Code, Sections 1151, 1152, and 1153.

199. Foreign Counterintelligence – Terrorism. Attorney General Guidelines on Foreign Counterintelligence. Executive Order 11905.

200. Foreign Counterintelligence Matters. Attorney General Guidelines on Foreign Counterintelligence. Executive Order 11905.

201. Foreign Counterintelligence Matters. Attorney General Guidelines on Foreign Counterintelligence. Executive Order 11905.

202. Foreign Counterintelligence Matters. Attorney General Guidelines on Foreign Counterintelligence. Executive Order 11905.

203. Foreign Counterintelligence Matters. Attorney General Guidelines on Foreign Counterintelligence. Executive Order 11905.

204. Federal Revenue Sharing. This classification covers FBI investigations conducted where the Attorney General has been authorized to bring civil action whenever he has reason to believe that a pattern or practice of discrimination in disbursement of funds under the Federal Revenue Sharing status exists.

205. Foreign Corrupt Practices Act of 1977. Title 15, United States Code, Section 78.

206. Fraud Against the Government – Department of Defense, Department of Agriculture, Department of Commerce, Community Services Organization, Department of Transportation. (See classification 46 (supra) for a statutory authority for this and the four following classifications.)

207. Fraud Against the Government-Environmental Protection Agency, National Aeronautics and Space Administration, Department of Energy, Department of Transportation.

208. Fraud Against the Government – General Services Administration.

209. Fraud Against the Government – Department of Health, and Human Services (Formerly, Department of Health, Education, and Welfare).

210. Fraud Against the Government – Department of Labor.

211. Ethics in Government Act of 1978, Title VI (Title 28, Sections 591-596).

212. Foreign Counterintelligence – Intelligence Community Support. This is an administrative classification for the FBI's operational and technical support to other Intelligence Community agencies.

213. Fraud Against the Government-Department of Education.

214. Civil Rights of Institutionalized Persons Act (Title 42, United States Code. Section 1997).

215. Foreign Counterintelligence Matters. Attorney General Guidelines on Foreign Counterintelligence. Executive Order 11905.

216. thru 229. Foreign Counterintelligence Matters. (Same authority as 215)

230. thru 240. FBI Training Matters.

241. DEA Applicant Investigations.

242. Automation Matters.

243. Intelligence Identities Protection Act of 1982.

244. Hostage Rescue Team.

245. Drug Investigative task Force.

246. thru 248. Foreign Counterintelligence Matters. (Same authority as 215)

249. Environmental Crimes-Investigations involving toxic or hazardous waste violations.

250. Tampering With Consumer Products (Title 18, U.S. Code, Section 1395)

251. Controlled Substance- Robbery;- Burglary (Title 18, U.S. Code, Section 2118)

252. Violent Crime Apprehension Program (VICAP). Case folders containing records relevant to the VICAP Program, in conjunction with the National Center for the Analysis of Violent Crime Record System at the FBI Academy; Quantico, Virginia. {PG 49161}

253. False Identification Crime Control Act of 1982 (Title 18, U.S. Code, Section 1028-Fraud and Related Activity in Connection With Identification Documents, and Section 1738-Mailing Private Identification Documents Without a Disclaimer)

254. Destruction of Energy Facilities (Title 18, U.S. Code, Section 1365) relates to the destruction of property of non-nuclear energy facilities.

255. Counterfeiting of State and Corporate Securities (Title 18, U.S. Code, Section 511) covers counterfeiting and forgery of all forms of what is loosely interpreted as securities.

256. Hostage Taking-Terrorism (Title 18, U.S. Code, Section 1203) prohibits taking of hostage(s) to compel third party to do or refrain from doing any act.

257. Trademark Counterfeiting Act (Title 18, United States Code, Section 2320) covers the international trafficking in goods which bear a counterfeited trademark.

258. Credit Card Fraud Act of 1984 (Title 18, United States Code, Section 1029) covers fraud and related activities in connection with access devices (credit and debit cards).

259. Security Clearance Investigations Program. (Same authority as 215)

260. Industrial Security Program. (Same authority as 215)

261. Security Officer Matters. (Same authority as 215)

262. Overseas Homicide (Attempted Homicide-International Terrorism. Title 18, United States Code, Section 2331.

263. Office of Professional Responsibility Matters.

264. Computer Fraud and Abuse Act of 1986. Electronic Communications Privacy Act of 1986. Title 18, United States Code, Section 1030; Title 18, United States Code, Section 2701.

265. Acts Terrorism in the United States – International Terrorist. (Followed by predicate offense from other classification.)

266. Acts of Terrorism in the United States – Domestic Terrorist. (Followed by predicate offense from other classification.)

267. Drug-Related Homicide. Title 21, U.S. Code, Section 848(e).

268. Engineering Technical Matters – FCI.

269. Engineering Technical Matters – Non-FCI.

270. Cooperative Witnesses.

271. Foreign Counterintelligence Matters. Attorney General Guidelines on Foreign Counterintelligence. Executive Order 11905.

272. Money Laundering. Title 18, U.S. Code, Sections 1956 and 1957.

273. Adoptive Forfeiture Matter – Drug. Forfeiture based on seizure of property by state, local or other Federal authority.

274. Adoptive Forfeiture Matter – Organized Crime. (Same explanation as 273.)

275. Adoptive Forfeiture Matter – White Collar Crime. (Same explanation as 273.)

276. Adoptive Forfeiture Matter – Violent Crime/Major Offenders Program. (Same explanation as 273.)

277. Adoptive Forfeiture Matter – Counterterrorism Program. (Same explanation as 273.)

RECORDS MAINTAINED IN THE FBI FIELD DIVISIONS -

FBI field divisions maintain for limited periods of time investigative, administrative and correspondence records, including files, index cards and related material, some of which are duplicated copies of reports and similar documents forwarded to FBI Headquarters. Most investigative activities conducted by FBI field divisions are reported to FBI Headquarters at one or more stages of the investigation. There are, however, investigative activities wherein no reporting was made to FBI Headquarters, e.g., pending cases not as yet reported and cases which were closed in the field division for any of a number of reasons without reporting to FBI Headquarters.

Duplicate records and records which extract information reported in the main files are also kept in the various divisions of the FBI to assist them in their day-to-day operation. These records are lists of individuals which contain certain biographic data, including physical description and photograph. They may also contain information concerning activities of the individual as reported to FBIHQ by the various field offices.

The establishment of these lists is necessitated by the needs of the Division to have immediate access to pertinent information duplicative of data found in the central records without the delay caused by a time-consuming manual search of central indices.

The manner of segregating these individuals varies depending on the particular needs of the FBI Division. The information pertaining to individuals who are a part of the list is derivative of information contained in the Central Records System. These duplicative records fall into the following categories:

(1) Listings of individuals used to assist in the location and apprehension of individuals for whom legal process is outstanding (fugitives):

(2) Listings of individuals used in the identification of particular offenders in cases where the FBI has jurisdiction. These listings include various photograph albums and background data concerning persons who have been formerly charged with a particular crime and who may be suspect in similar criminal activities; and photographs of individuals who are unknown but suspected of involvement in a particular criminal activity, for example, bank surveillance photographs:

(3) Listings of individuals as part of an overall criminal intelligence effort by the FBI. This would include photograph albums, lists of individuals known to be involved in criminal activity, including theft from interstate shipment, interstate transportation of stolen property, and individuals in the upper echelon of organized crime:

(4) Listings of individuals in connection with the FBI's mandate to carry out Presidential directives on January 8, 1943, July 24, 1950. December 15, 1953, and February 18, 1976, which designated the FBI to carry out investigative work in matters relating to espionage, sabotage, and foreign counterintelligence. These listings may include photograph albums and other listings containing biographic data regarding individuals. This would include lists of identified and suspected foreign intelligence agents and informants:

(5) Special indices duplicative of the central indices used to access the Central Records System have been created from time to time in conjunction with the administration and investigation of major cases. This duplication and segregation facilitates access to documents prepared in connection with major cases.

In recent years, as the emphasis on the investigation of white collar crime, organized crime, and hostile foreign intelligence operations has increased, the FBI has been confronted with increasingly complicated cases, which require more intricate information processing capabilities. Since these complicated investigations frequently involve massive volumes of evidence and other investigative information, the FBI uses its computers, when necessary to collate, analyze, and retrieve investigative information in the most accurate and expeditious manner possible. It should be noted that this computerized investigative information, which is extracted from the main files or other commercial or governmental sources, is only maintained as necessary to support the FBI's investigative activities. Information from these internal computerized subsystems of the "Central Records System" {PG 49162} is not accessed by any other agency. All disclosures of computerized information are made in printed form in accordance with the routine uses which are set forth below.

Records also are maintained on a temporary basis relevant to the FBI's domestic police cooperating program, where assistance in obtaining information is provided to state and local police agencies.

Also, personnel type information, dealing with such matters as attendance and production and accuracy requirements is maintained by some divisions.

CENTRAL FILES INDICES

The following table identifies various listings or indexes maintained by the FBI which have been or are being used by various divisions of the FBI in their day-to-day operations. The chart identifies the list by name, description and use, and where maintained, i.e. FBI Headquarters and/or Field Office. The number in parentheses in the field office column indicates the number of field offices which maintain these indices.

The chart indicates, under "status of index," those indexes which are in current use (designated by the word "active") and those which are no longer being used, although maintained (designated by the word "inactive"). There are 27 separate indices which are classified in accordance with existing regulations and are not included in this chart.

The following indices are no longer being used by the FBI and are being maintained at FBIHQ pending receipt of authority to destroy: Black Panther Party Photo Index; Black United Front Index; Security Index; and Wounded Knee Album.

FBI CENTRAL FILE INDICES

Title of index: Administrative Index (ADEX)

Description and use:

Consists of cards with descriptive data on individuals who were subject to investigation in a national emergency because they were believed to constitute a potential or active threat to the internal security of the United States. When ADEX was started in 1971, it was made up of people who were formerly on the Security Index, Reserve Index, and Agitator Index. This index is maintained in two separate locations in FBI Headquarters. ADEX was discontinued in January 1978

Status of index: Inactive

Maintained at Headquarters Yes

Maintained at field office Yes (29).

Title of index: Anonymous Letter File

Description and use:

Consists of photographs of anonymous communications and extorionate credit transactions, kidnapping, extortion and threatening letters.

Status of index: Active

Maintained at Headquarters Yes

Maintained at field office No.

Title of index: Associates of DEA Class 1 Narcotics Violators Listing

Description and use:

Consists of a computer listing of individuals whom DEA has identified as associates of Class 1 Narcotics Violators.

Status of index: Active

Maintained at Headquarters Yes

Maintained at field office Yes (56).

Title of index: Background Investigation Index-Department of Justice

Description and use:

Consists of cards on persons who have been the subject of a full field investigation in connection with their consideration for employment in sensitive positions with Department of Justice, such as U.S. Attorney, Federal judges, or a high level Department position.

Status of index: Active

Maintained at Headquarters Yes
Maintained at field office No.

Title of index: Background Investigation Index-White House, Other Executive Agencies, and Congress

Description and use:

Consists of cards on persons who have been the subject of a full field investigation in connection with their consideration for employment in sensitive positions with the White House, Executive agencies (other than the Department of Justice) and the Congress.

Status of index: Active

Maintained at Headquarters Yes
Maintained at field office No.

Title of index: Bank Fraud and Embezzlement Index

Description and use:

Consists of individuals who have been the subject of ''Bank Fraud and Embezzlement'' investigation. This file is used as an investigative aid.

Status of index: Active

Maintained at Headquarters No
Maintained at field office Yes (1).

Title of index: Bank Robbery Album

Description and use:

Consists of photos of bank robbers, burglars, and larceny subjects. In some field offices at will also contain pictures obtained from local police departments of known armed robbers and thus potential bank robbers. The index is used to develop investigative leads in bank robbery cases and may also be used to show to witnesses of bank robberies. It is usually filed by race, height, and age. This index is also maintained in one resident agency (a suboffice of a field office)

Status of index: Active

Maintained at Headquarters No

Maintained at field office Yes (47).

Title of index: Bank Robbery Nickname index

Description and use

Consists of nicknames used by known bank robbers. The index card on each would contain the real name and method of operation and are filed in alphabetical order

Status of index: Active

Maintained at Headquarters No

Maintained at field office Yes (1).

Title of index: Bank Robbery Note File

Description and use:

Consists of photographs of notes used in bank robberies in which the suspect has been identified. This index is used to help solve robberies in which the subject has not been identified but a note was left. The role is compared with the index to try to match the sentence structure and handwriting for the purpose of identifying possible suspects.

Status of index: Active

Maintained at Headquarters Yes

Maintained at field office No.

Title of index: Bank Robbery Suspect Index

Description and use:

Consists of a control file or index cards with photos, if available, of bank robbers or burglars. In some field offices these people may be part of the bank robbery album. This index is generally maintained and used in the same manner as the bank robbery album

Status of index: Active

Maintained at Headquarters No

Maintained at field office Yes (33).

Title of index: Car Ring Case Photo Album

Description and use:

Consists of photos of subjects and suspects involved in a large car theft ring investigation. It is used as an investigative aid.

Status of index: Active

Maintained at Headquarters No

Maintained at field office Yes (3).

Title of index: Car Ring Case Photo Album and Index

Description and use:

Consists of photos of subjects and suspects involved in a large car theft ring investigation. The card index maintained in addition to the photo album contains the names and addresses appearing on fraudulent title histories for stolen vehicles. Most of these names appearing on these titles are fictitious. But the photo album and card indexes are used as an investigative aid.

Status of index: Active

Maintained at Headquarters No

Maintained at field office Yes (1)

Title of index: Car Ring Case Toll Call Index

Description and use:

Consists of cards with information on persons who subscribe to telephone numbers to which toll calls have been placed by the major subjects of a large car theft ring investigation. It is maintained numerically by telephone number. It is used to facilitate the development of probably cause for a court-approved wiretap.

Status of index: Active

Maintained at Headquarters No

Maintained at field office Yes (2)

Title of index: Car Ring Theft Working Index

Description and use:

Contains cards on individuals involved in car ring theft cases on which the FBI Laboratory is doing examination work.

Status of index: Active

Maintained at Headquarters Yes

Maintained at field office No.

Title of index: Cartage Album

Description and use:

Consists of photos with descriptive data of individuals who have been convicted of theft from interstate shipment or interstate transportation of stolen property where there is a reason to believe they may repeat the offense. It is used in investigating the above violations.

Status of index: Active

Maintained at Headquarters No

Maintained at field office Yes (3).

Title of index: Channelizing Index

Description and use:

Consists of cards with the names and case file numbers of people who are frequently mentioned in information reports. The index is used to facilitate the distributing or channeling of informant reports to appropriate files.

Status of index: Active

Maintained at Headquarters No

Maintained at field office Yes (9)

Title of index: Check Circular File

Description and use:

Consists of fliers numerically in a control file on fugitives who are notorious fradulent check passers and who are engaged in a continuing operation of passing checks. The fliers which include the subject's name, photo, a summary of the subject's method of operation and other identifying data is used to alert other FBI field offices and business establishments which may be the victims of bad checks.

Status of index: Active

Maintained at Headquarters Yes

Maintained at field office Yes (43).

Title of index: Computerized Telephone Number File (CTNF) Intelligence

Description and use:

Consists of a computer listing of telephone numbers (and subscribers' names and addresses) utilized by subjects and/or certain individuals which come to the FBI's attention during major investigations. During subsequent investigations, telephone numbers, obtained through subpoena, are matched with the telephone numbers on file to determine connections or associations

Status of index: Active

Maintained at Headquarters Yes

Maintained at field office No.

Title of index: Con Man Index

Description and use:

Consists of computerized names of individuals, along with company affiliation, who travel nationally and internationally while participating in large-dollar-value financial swindles.

Status of index: Active

Maintained at Headquarters Yes

Maintained at field office No.

Title of index: Confidence Game (Flim Flam) Album

Description and use:

Consists of photos with descriptive information on individuals who have been arrested for confidence games and related activities. It is used as an investigative aid.

Status of index: Active

Maintained at Headquarters No

Maintained at field office Yes (4).

Title of index: Copyright Matters Index

Description and use:

Consists of cards of individuals who are film collectors and film titles. It is used as a reference in the investigation of copyright matters.

Status of index: Active

Maintained at Headquarters No

Maintained at field office Yes (1).

Title of index: Criminal Intelligence Index

Description and use:

Consists of cards with name and file number of individuals who have become the subject of an antiracketeering investigation. The index is used as a quick way to ascertain file numbers and the correct spelling of names. This index is also maintained in one resident agency.

Status of index: Active

Maintained at Headquarters No

Maintained at field office Yes (2).

Title of index: Criminal Informant Index

Description and use:

Consists of cards containing identity and brief background information on all active and inactive informants furnishing information in the criminal area.

Status of index: Active

Maintained at Headquarters Yes

Maintained at field office No.

Title of index: DEA Class 1 Narcotics Violators Listing

Description and use:

Consists of a computer listing of narcotic violators-persons known to manufacture, supply, or distribute large quantities of illicit drugs-with background data. It is used by the FBI in their role of assisting DEA in disseminating intelligence data concerning illicit drug trafficking. This index is also maintained in two resident agencies.

Status of index: Active

Maintained at Headquarters Yes

Maintained at field office Yes (56).

Title of index: Deserter Index

Description and use:

Contains cards with the names of individuals who are known military deserters. It is used as an investigative aid.

Status of index: Active

Maintained at Headquarters No

Maintained at field office Yes (4).

Title of index: False Identities Index

Description and use:

Contains cards with the names of deceased individuals whose birth certificates have been obtained by other persons for possible false identification uses and in connection with which the FBI laboratory has been requested to perform examinations.

Status of index: Inactive

Maintained at Headquarters Yes

Maintained at field office No.

Title of index: False Identities List

Description and use:

Consist of a listing of names of deceased individuals whose birth certificates have been obtained after the person's death, and thus whose names are possibly being used for false identification purposes. The listing is maintained as part of the FBI's program to find persons using false identities for illegal purposes.

Status of index: Inactive

Maintained at Headquarters No

Maintained at field office Yes (31).

Title of index: False Identity Photo Album

Description and use:

Consists of names and photos of people who have been positively identified as using a false identification. This is used as an investigative aid in the FBI's investigation of false identities.

Status of index: Inactive

Maintained at Headquarters No

Maintained at field office Yes (2).

Title of index: FBI/Inspector General (IG) Case Pointer System (FICPS)

Description and use:

Consists of computerized listing of individual names of organizations which are the subject of active and inactive fraud investigations, along with the name of the agency conducting the investigation. Data is available to IG offices throughout the federal government to prevent duplication of investigative activity.

Status of index: Active

Maintained at Headquarters Yes

Maintained at field office No.

Title of index: FBI Wanted Persons Index

Description and use:

Consists of cards on persons being sought on the basis of Federal warrants covering violations which fall under the jurisdiction of the FBI. It is used as a ready reference to identify those fugitives.

Status of index: Active

Maintained at Headquarters Yes
Maintained at field office No.

Title of index: Foreign Counterintelligence (FCI)

Description and use:

Consists of cards with identity background data on all active and inactive operational and informational assets in the foreign counterintelligence field. It is used as a reference aid on the FCI Asset program.

Status of index: Active

Maintained at Headquarters Yes
Maintained at field office No.

Title of index: Fraud Against the Government Index

Description and use:

Consists of individuals who have been the subject of a ''fraud against the Government'' investigation. It is used as investigative aid

Status of index: Active

Maintained at Headquarters No
Maintained at field office Yes (1).

Title of index: Fugitive Bank Robbers File

Description and use:

Consists of fliers on bank robbery fugitives filed sequentially in a control file. FBI Headquarters distributes to the field offices fliers on bank robbers in a fugitive status for 15 or more days to facilitate their location.

Status of index: Active

Maintained at Headquarters Yes
Maintained at field office Yes (43).

Title of index: General Security Index

Description and use:

Contains cards on all persons that have been the subject of a security classification investigation by the FBI field office. These cards are used for general reference purposes.

Status of index: Active

Maintained at Headquarters No

Maintained at field office Yes (1).

Title of index: Hoodlum License Plate Index

Description and use:

Consists of cards with the license plates numbers and descriptive data on known hoodlums and cars observed in the vicinity of hoodlum homes. It is used for quick identifica-tion of such person in the course of investigation. The one index which is not fully retrievable in maintained by a resident agency.

Status of index: Active

Maintained at Headquarters No

Maintained at field office Yes (3).

Title of index: Identification Order Fugitive Flier File

Description and use:

Consists of fliers numerically in a control file. When immediate leads have been exhausted in fugitive investigations and a crime of considerable public interest has been committed, the fliers are given wide circulation among law enforcement agencies throughout the United States and are posted in post offices. The fliers contain the fugitive's photograph, fingerprints, and description.

Status of index: Active

Maintained at Headquarters Yes

Maintained at field office Yes (49).

Title of index: Informant Index

Description and use:

Consists of cards with the name, symbol numbers, and brief background information on the following categories of active and inactive informants, top echelon criminal informants, security informants, criminal information, operational and informational assets, extremist informants (discontinued), plant informants, informants on and about certain military bases (discontinued), and potential criminal informants.

Status of index: Active

Maintained at Headquarters No

Maintained at field office Yes (56).

Title of index: Informants in Other Field offices, Index of

Description and use:

Consist of cards with names and/or symbol numbers of informants in other FBI field offices that are in a position to furnish information that would also be included on the index card.

Status of index: Active

Maintained at Headquarters No

Maintained at field office Yes (15).

Title of index: Interstate Transportation of Stolen Aircraft Photo Album

Description and use:

Consists of photos and descriptive data on individuals who are suspects known to have been involved in interstate transportation of stolen aircraft. It is used as an investigative aid.

Status of index: Active

Maintained at Headquarters No

Maintained at field office Yes (1).

Title of index: IRS Wanted List

Description and use:

Consists of one-page fliers from IRS on individuals with background information who are wanted by IRS for tax purposes. It is used in the identification of persons wanted by IRS

Status of index: Active

Maintained at Headquarters No

Maintained at field office Yes (11).

Title of index: Kidnapping Book

Description and use:

Consists of data, filed chronologically, on kidnappings that have occurred since the early fifties. The victims' names and the suspects, if known, would be listed with a brief description of the circumstances surrounding the kidnapping. The file is used as a reference aid in matching up prior methods of operation in unsolved kidnapping cases

Status of index: Active

Maintained at Headquarters Yes

Maintained at field office No (4).

Title of index: Known Check Passers Album

Description and use:

Consists of photos with descriptive data of persons known to pass stolen, forged, or counterfeit checks. It is used as an investigative aid

Status of index: Active

Maintained at Headquarters No

Maintained at field office Yes (4).

Title of index: Known Gambler Index

Description and use:

Consists of cards with names, descriptive data, and sometimes photos of individuals who are known bookmakers and gamblers. The index is used in organized crime and gambling. investigations. Subsequent to GAO's review, and at the recommendation of the inspection team at one of the two field offices where the index was destroyed and thus is not included in the total.

Status of index: Active

Maintained at Headquarters No

Maintained at field office Yes (5).

Title of index: La Cosa Nostra (LCN) Membership Index

Description and use:

Contains cards on individuals having been identified as members of the LCN index. The cards contain personal data and pictures. The index is used solely by FBI agents for assistance in investigating organized crime matters

Status of index: Active

Maintained at Headquarters Yes
Maintained at field office Yes (55).

Title of index: Leased Line Letter Request Index

Description and use:

Contains cards on individuals and organizations who are or have been the subject of a national security electronic surveillance where a leased line letter was necessary. It is used as an administrative and statistical aid.

Status of index: Active

Maintained at Headquarters Yes
Maintained at field office No.

Title of index: Mail Cover Index

Description and use:

Consists of cards containing a record of all mail covers conducted on individuals and groups since about January 1973. It is used for reference in preparing mail cover requests.

Status of index: Active

Maintained at Headquarters Yes
Maintained at field office No.

Title of index: Military Deserter Index

Description and use:

Consists of cards containing the names of all military deserters where the various military branches have requested FBI assistance in locating. It is used as an administrative aid.

Status of index: Active

Maintained at Headquarters Yes
Maintained at field office No.

Title of index: National Bank Robbery Album

Description and use:

Consists of fliers on bank robbery suspects held sequentially in a control file. When an identifiable bank camera photograph is available and the case has been under investigation for 30 days without identifying the subject, FBIHQ sends a flier to the field offices to help identify the subject.

Status of index: Active

Maintained at Headquarters Yes

Maintained at field office Yes (42).

Title of index: National Fraudulent Check File

Description and use:

Contains photographs of the signature on stolen and counterfeit checks. It is filed alphabetically but there is no way of knowing the names are real or fictitious. The index is used to help solve stolen check cases by matching checks obtained in such cases against the index to identify a possible suspect.

Status of index: Active

Maintained at Headquarters Yes

Maintained at field office No.

Title of index: National Security Electronic Surveillance Card File

Description and use:

Contains cards recording electronic surveillances previously authorized by the Attorney General and previously and currently authorized by the FISC; current and previous assets in the foreign counterintelligence field; and a historical, inactive section which contains cards believed to record nonconserted physical entries in national security cases, previously toll billings, mail covers and leased lines. The inactive section also contains cards reflecting previous Attorney General approvals and denials for warrantless electronic surveillance in the national security cases.

Status of index: Inactive

Maintained at Headquarters Yes

Maintained at field office No.

Title of index: Night Depository Trap Index

Description and use:

Contains cards with the names of persons who have been involved in the theft of deposits made in bank night depository boxes. Since these thefts have involved various methods, the FBI uses the index to solve such cases by matching up similar methods to identify possible suspects

Status of index: Active

Maintained at Headquarters Yes

Maintained at field office No.

Title of index: Organized Crime Photo Album

Description and use:

Consists of photos and background information on individuals involved in organized crime activities. The index is used as a ready reference in identifying organized crime figures within the field offices' jurisdiction.

Status of index: Active

Maintained at Headquarters No

Maintained at field office Yes (13).

Title of index: Photospread Identification Elimination File

Description and use:

Consists of photos of individuals who have been subjects and suspects in FBI investigations. It also includes photos received from other law enforcement agencies. These pictures can be used to show witnesses of certain crimes.

Status of index: Active

Maintained at Headquarters No

Maintained at field office Yes (14).

Title of index: Prostitute Photo Album

Description and use:

Consists of photos with background data on prostitutes who have prior local or Federal arrests for prostitution. It is used to identify prostitutes in connection with investigations under the White Slave Traffic Act

Status of index: Active

Maintained at Headquarters No

Maintained at field office Yes (4).

Title of index: Royal Canadian Mounted Policy (RCMP) Wanted Circular File

Description and use:
Consists of a control file of individuals with background information of persons wanted by the RCMP. It is used to notify the RCMP if an individual is located.

Status of index: Active

Maintained at Headquarters No
Maintained at field office Yes (17).

Title of index: Security Informant Index

Description and use:
Consists of cards containing identity and brief background information on all active and inactive informants furnishing information in the criminal area.

Status of index: Active

Maintained at Headquarters Yes
Maintained at field office No.

Title of index: Security Subjects Control Index

Description and use:
Consists of cards containing the names and case file numbers of individuals who have been subject to security investigations check. It is used as a reference source.

Status of index: Active

Maintained at Headquarters No
Maintained at field office Yes (1).

Title of index: Security Telephone Number Index

Description and use:
Contains cards with telephone subscriber information subpoenaed from the telephone company in any security investigation. It is maintained numerically by the last three digits in the telephone number. It is used for general reference purposes in security investigations.

Status of index: Active

Maintained at Headquarters No
Maintained at field office Yes (1).

Title of index: Selective Service Violators Index

Description and use:

Contains cards on individuals being sought on the basis of Federal warrants for violation of the Selective Service Act

Status of index: Active

Maintained at Headquarters Yes

Maintained at field office No.

Title of index: Sources of Information Index

Description and use:

Consist of cards on individuals and organizations such as banks, motels, local government that are willing to furnish information to the FBI with sufficient frequency to justify listing for the benefit of all agents. It is maintained to facilitate the use of such sources.

Status of index: Active

Maintained at Headquarters No

Maintained at field office Yes (10).

Title of index: Special Services Index

Description and use:

Contains cards of prominent individuals who are in a position to furnish assistance in connection with FBI investigative responsibility.

Status of index: Active

Maintained at Headquarters No

Maintained at field office Yes (28).

Title of index: Stolen Checks and Fraud by Wire Index

Description and use:

Consists of cards on individuals involved in check and fraud by wire violations. It is used as an investigative aid.

Status of index: Active

Maintained at Headquarters No

Maintained at field office Yes (1).

Title of index: Stop Notices Index

Description and use

Consists of cards on names of subjects or property where the field office has placed a stop at another law enforcement agency or private business such as pawn shops in the event information comes to the attention of that agency concerning the subject or property. This is filed numerically by investigative classification. It is used to insure that the agency where the stop is placed is notified when the subject is apprehended or the property is located or recovered.

Status of index: Active

Maintained at Headquarters No

Maintained at field office Yes (43).

Title of index: Surveillance Locator Index

Description and use:

Consists of cards with basic data on individuals and businesses which have come under physical surveillance in the city in which the field office is located. It is used for general reference purposes in antiracketeering investigations.

Status of index: Active

Maintained at Headquarters No

Maintained at field office Yes (2).

Title of index: Telephone Number Index-Gamblers

Description and use

Contains information on persons identified usually as a result of a subpoena for the names of subscribers to particular telephone numbers or toll records for a particular phone number of area gamblers and bookmakers. The index cards are filed by the last three digits of the telephone number. The index in used gambling investigations.

Status of index: Active

Maintained at Headquarters No

Maintained at field office Yes (2).

Title of index: Telephone Subscriber and Toll Records Check Index

Description and use:

Contains cards with information on persons identified as the result of a formal request or subpoena to the phone company for the identity of subscribers to particular telephone numbers. The index cards are filed by telephone number and would also include identity of the subscriber, billing party's identity, subscriber's address, date of request from the telephone company, and file number.

Status of index: Active

Maintained at Headquarters No

Maintained at field office Yes (1).

Title of index: Thieves, Couriers and Fences Photo Index

Description and use:

Consists of photos and background information on individuals who are or are suspected of being thieves, couriers, or fences based on their past activity in the area of interstate transportation of stolen property. It is used as an investigative aid.

Status of index: Active

Maintained at Headquarters No

Maintained at field office Yes (4).

Title of index: Toll Record Request Index

Description and use:

Contains cards on individuals and organizations on whom toll records have been obtained in national security related cases and with respect to which FBIHQ had to prepare a request letter. It is used primarily to facilitate the handling of repeat requests on individuals listed

Status of index: Active

Maintained at Headquarters Yes

Maintained at field office No.

Title of index: Top Burglar Album

Description and use:

Consists of photos and background data of known and suspect top burglars involved in the area of interstate transportation of stolen property. It is used as an investigative aid.

Status of index: Active

Maintained at Headquarters No
Maintained at field office Yes (4).

Title of index: Top Echelon Criminal Informer Program (TECIP) Index

Description and use:

Consists of cards containing identity and brief background information on individuals who are either furnishing high level information in the organized crime area or are under development to furnish such information. The index is used primarily to evaluate, corroborate, and coordinate informant information and to develop prosecutive data against racket figures under Federal, State, and local statutes.

Status of index: Active

Maintained at Headquarters Yes
Maintained at field office No.

Title of index: Top Ten Program File

Description and use:

Consists of fliers, filed numerically in a control file, on fugitives considered by the FBI to be 1 of the 10 most wanted. Including a fugitive of the top 10 usually assures a greater national news coverage as well as nation-wide circulation of the flier.

Status of index: Active

Maintained at Headquarters Yes
Maintained at field office Yes (44).

Title of index: Top Thief Program Index

Description and use:

Consists of cards of individuals who are professional burglars, robbers, or fences dealing in items likely to be passed in interstate commerce or who travel interstate to commit the crime. Usually photographs and background information would also be obtained on the index card. The index is used as an investigative aid.

Status of index: Active

Maintained at Headquarters No
Maintained at field office Yes (27).

Title of index: Truck Hijack Photo Album

Description and use:

Contains photos and descriptive data of individuals who are suspected truck hijackers. It is used as an investigative aid and for displaying photos to witnesses and/or victims to identify unknown subjects in hijacking cases.

Status of index: Active

Maintained at Headquarters No
Maintained at field office Yes (4).

Title of index: Truck Thief Suspect Photo Album

Description and use:

Consists of photos and background data on individuals previously arrested or are currently suspects regarding vehicle theft. The index is used as an investigative aid.

Status of index: Active

Maintained at Headquarters No
Maintained at field office Yes (1).

Title of index: Traveling Criminal Photo Album

Description and use:

Consists of photos with identifying data of individuals convicted of various criminal offenses and may be suspects in other offenses. It is used as an investigative aid.

Status of index: Active

Maintained at Headquarters No
Maintained at field office Yes (1).

Title of index: Veterans Administrative (VA)/Federal Housing Administration Matters (FHA) Index

Description and use:

Consists of cards of individuals who have been subject of an investigation relative to VA and FHA matters. It is used as an investigative aid.

Status of index: Active

Maintained at Headquarters No
Maintained at field office Yes (1).

Title of index: Wanted Fliers File

Description and use:

Consists of fliers, filed numerically in a control file, on badly wanted fugitives whose apprehension may be facilitated by a flier. The flier contains the names, photographs, aliases, previous convictions, and a caution notice

Status of index: Active

Maintained at Headquarters Yes
Maintained at field office Yes (46).

Title of index: Wheeldex

Description and use

Contains the nicknames and the case file numbers of organized crime members. It is used in organized crime investigations

Status of index: Active

Maintained at Headquarters No

Maintained at field office Yes (1).

Title of index: White House Special Index

Description and use:

Contains cards on all potential White House appointees, staff members, guests, and visitors that have been referred to the FBI by the White House security office for a records check to identify any adverse or derogatory information. This index is used to expedite such check in view of the tight timeframe usually required.

Status of index: Active

Maintained at Headquarters Yes

Maintained at field office No.

Title of index: Witness Protection Program Index

Description and use:

Contains cards on individuals who have been furnished a new identity by the U.S. Justice Department because of their testimony in organized crime trials. It is used primarily to notify the U.S. Marshals Service when information related to the safety of a protected witness comes to the FBI's attention.

Status of index: Active

Maintained at Headquarters Yes

Maintained at field office No.

AUTHORITY FOR MAINTENANCE OF THE SYSTEM:

Federal Records Act of 1950, Title 44, United States Code, chapter 31, section 3101; and title 36, Code of Federal Regulations, chapter XII, require Federal agencies to insure that adequate and proper records are made and preserved to document the organization, functions, policies, decisions, procedures and transactions and to protect the legal and financial rights of the Federal Government, title 28, United States Code, section 534, delegates authority to the Attorney General to acquire, collect, classify, and preserve identification, criminal identification, crime and other records.

ROUTINE USES OF RECORDS MAINTAINED IN THE SYSTEM;

(Including categories of users and the purposes of such uses)

Records, both investigative and administrative, are maintained in this system in order to permit the FBI to function efficiently as an authority, responsive component of the Department of Justice. Therefore, information in this system is disclosed to officials and employees of the Department of Justice, and/or all components thereof, who have need of the information in the performance of their official duties.

Personal information from this system may be disclosed as a routine use to any Federal agency where the purpose in making the disclosure is compatible with the law enforcement purpose for which it was collected, e.g., to assist the recipient agency in conducting a lawful criminal or intelligence investigation, to assist the recipient agency in making a determination concerning an individual's suitability for employment and/or trustworthiness for employment and/or trustworthiness for access clearance purposes, or to assist the recipient agency in the performance of any authorized function where access to records in this system is declared by the recipient agency to be relevant to that function.

In addition, personal information may be disclosed from this system to members of the Judicial Branch of the Federal Government in response to a specific request, or at the initiation of the FBI, where disclosure appears relevant to the authorized function of the recipient judicial office or court system. An example would be where an individual is being considered for employment by a Federal judge.

Information in this system may be disclosed as a routine use to any state or local government agency directly engaged in the criminal justice process, e.g., police, prosecution, penal, probation and parole, and the judiciary, where access is directly related to a law enforcement function of the recipient agency e.g. in connection with a lawful criminal or intelligence investigation, or making a determination concerning an individual's suitability for employment as a state or local law enforcement employee or concerning a victim's compensation under a state statute. Disclosure to a state or local government agency, (a) not directly engaged in the criminal justice process or (b) for a licensing or regulatory function, is considered on an individual basis only under exceptional circumstances, as determined by the FBI.

Information in this system pertaining to the use, abuse or traffic of controlled substances may be disclosed as a routine use to federal, state or local law enforcement agencies and to licensing or regulatory agencies empowered to engage in the institution and prosecution of cases before courts and licensing boards in matters relating to controlled substances, including courts and licensing boards responsible for the licensing or certification of individuals in the fields of pharmacy and medicine.

Information in this system may be disclosed as a routine use in a proceeding before a court or adjudicative body, e.g., the Equal Employment Opportunity Commission and the Merit Systems Protection Board, before which the FBI is authorized to appear, when (a) the FBI or any employee thereof in his or her official capacity, or (b) any employee in his or her individual capacity where the Department of Justice has agreed to represent the employee, or (c) the United States, where the FBI determines it is likely to be affected by the litigation, is a party to litigation or has an interest in litigation and such records are determined by the FBI to be relevant to the litigation.

Information in this system may be disclosed as a routine use to an organization or individual in both the public or private sector if deemed necessary to elicit information or cooperation from the recipient for use by the FBI in the performance of an authorized activity. An example would be where the activities of an individual are disclosed to a member of the public in order to elicit his/her assistance in our apprehension or detection efforts.

Information in this system may be disclosed as a routine use to an organization or individual in both the public or private sector where there is reason to believe the recipient is or could become the target of a particular criminal activity or conspiracy, to the extent the information is relevant to the protection of life or property.

Information in this system may be disclosed to legitimate agency of a foreign government where the FBI determines that the information is relevant to that agency's responsibilities, and dissemination {PG 49169} serves the best interests of the U.S. Government, and where the purpose in making the disclosure is compatible with the purpose for which the information was collected.

Relevant information may be disclosed from this system to the news media and general public where there exists a legitimate public interest, e.g., to assist in the location of Federal fugitives, to provide notification of arrests, and where necessary for protection from imminent threat of life or property. This would include releases of information in accordance with 28 CFR 50.2.

A record relating to an actual or potential civil or criminal violation of the copyright statute, Title 17, United States Code, or the trademark statutes. Titles 15 and 17, U.S. Code, may be disseminated to a person injured by such violation to assist him/her in the institution or maintenance of a suit brought under such titles.

The FBI has received inquiries from private citizens and Congressional offices on behalf of constituents seeking assistance in locating individuals such as missing children and heirs to estates. Where the need is acute, and where it appears FBI files may be the only lead in locating the individual, consideration will be given to furnishing relevant information to the requester. Information will be provided only in those instances where there are reasonable grounds to conclude from available information the individual being sought would want the information to be furnished, e.g., an heir to a large estate. Information with regard to missing children will not be provided where they have reached their majority.

Information contained in this system, may be made available to a Member of Congress or staff acting upon the member's behalf when the member of staff requests the information in behalf of and at the request of the individual who is the subject of the record.

A record from this system of records may be disclosed as a routine use to the National Archives and Records Administration and General Services Administration in records management inspections conducted under the authority of 44 U.S.C. 2904 and 2906, to the extent that legislation governing the records permits.

POLICIES AND PRACTICES FOR STORING, RETRIEVING, ACCESSING, RETAINING, AND DISPOSING OF RECORDS IN THE SYSTEM:

STORAGE:

The active main files are maintained in hard copy form and some inactive records are maintained on microfilm. Investigative information which is maintained in computerized form may be stored in memory, on disk storage, on computer tape, or on a computer printed listing.

RETRIEVABLITY:

The FBI General Index must be searched to determine what information, if any, the FBI may have in its files. Index records, or pointers to specific FBI files, are created on all manner of subject matters, but the predominant type record is the name index record. It should be noted the FBI does not index all individuals who furnish information or all names developed during the course of an investigation. Only that information considered pertinent, relevant, or essential for future retrieval,is indexed. In certain major cases, individuals interviewed may be indexed to facilitate the administration of the investigation. The FBI has automated that portion of its index containing the most recent information-15 years for criminal related matters and 30 years for intelligence and other type matters. Automation will not change the "Central Records System"; it will only facilitate more economic and expeditious access to the main files.

Searches against the automated records are accomplished on a "batch off-line" basis for certain submitting agencies where the name search requests conform to FBI specified formats and also in an "on-line" mode with the use of video display terminals for other requests. The FBI will not permit any organization, public or private, outside the FBI to have direct access to the FBI indices system. All searches against the indices data base will be performed on site within FBI space by FBI personnel with the assistance of the automated procedures, where feasible.

Automation of the various FBI field office indices was completed in 1989. This automation initiative has been on a "day-one" basis. This indices system points to specific files within a given field office. Additionally, certain complicated investigative matters may be supported by specialized computer systems or by individual microcomputers. Indices created in these environments are maintained as part of the particular computer system and accessible only through the system or through printed listings of the indices. Full text retrieval is used in a limited number of cases as an investigative technique. It is not part of the normal search process and is not used as a substitute for the General Index or computer indices mentioned above.

The FBI will transfer historical records to the National Archives consistent with 44 U.S.C. 2103. No record of individuals or subject matter will be retained for transferred files; however, a record of the file numbers will be retained to provide full accountability of FBI files and thus preserve the integrity of the filing system.

SAFEGUARDS:

Records are maintained in a restricted area and are accessed only by agency personnel. All FBI employees receive a complete background investigation prior to being hired. All employees are cautioned about divulging confidential information or any information contained in FBI files. Failure to abide by this provision violates Department of Justice regulations and may violate certain statutes providing maximum severe penalties of a ten thousand dollar fine or 10 years imprisonment or both. Employees who resign or retire are also cautioned about divulging information acquired in the jobs.

Registered mail is used to transmit routine hard copy records between field offices. Highly classified records are hand carried by Special Agents or personnel of the Armed Forces Courier Service. Highly classified or sensitive privacy information, which is electronically transmitted between field offices, is transmitted in encrypted form to prevent interception and interpretation. Information transmitted in teletype form is placed in the main files of both the receiving and transmitting field offices. Field offices involved in certain complicated investigative matters may be provided with on-line access to the duplicative computerized information which is maintained for them on disk storage in the FBI Computer Center in Washington, D.C., and this computerized data is also transmitted in encrypted form.

RETENTION AND DISPOSAL:

As the result of an extensive review of FBI records conducted by NARA, records evaluated as historical and permanent will be transferred to the National Archives after established retention periods and administrative needs of the FBI have elapsed. As deemed necessary, certain records may be subject to restricted examination and usage, as provided by 44 U.S.C. section 2104.

FBI record disposition programs relevant to this System are conducted in accordance with the FBI Records Retention Plan and Disposition Schedule which was approved by the Archivist of the United States and the U.S. District Court, District of Columbia. {PG 49170} Investigative, applicant and administrative records which meet the destruction criteria will be destroyed after 20 or 30 years at FBI Headquarters and after 1, 5, 10 or 20 years in FBI Field Offices. Historical records will be transferred to the National Archives after 30 or 50 years, contingent upon investigative and administrative needs. The administrative indices and listings described within this System were appraised separately and disposition authority established. (Job No. NC1-65-82-4 and amendments)

SYSTEM MANAGER(S) AND ADDRESS:

Director, Federal Bureau of Investigation
Washington, DC 20535.

NOTIFICATION PROCEDURE:

Same as above.

RECORD ACCESS PROCEDURES:

A request for access to a record from the system shall be made in writing with the envelope and the letter clearly marked "Privacy Access Request". Include in the request your full name, complete address, date of birth, place of birth, notarized signature, and other identifying data you may wish to furnish to assist in making a proper search of our records. Also include the general subject matter of the document or its file number. The requester will also provide a return address for transmitting the information. Requests for access to information maintained at FBI Headquarters must be addressed to the Director, Federal Bureau of Investigation, Washington, DC 20535. Requests for information maintained at FBI field divisions or Legal Attachés must be made separately and addressed to the specific field division or Legal Attaché listed in the appendix to this system notice.

RECORD CONTESTING PROCEDURES:

Individuals desiring to contest or amend information maintained in the system should also direct their request to the Director, Federal Bureau of Investigation, Washington, DC 20535, stating clearly and concisely what information is being contested, the reasons for contesting it, and the proposed amendment to the information sought.

RECORD SOURCE CATEGORIES:

The FBI, by the very nature and requirement to investigate violations of law within its investigative jurisdiction and its responsibility for the internal security of the United States, collects information from a wide variety of sources. Basically, it is the result of investigative efforts and information furnished by other Government agencies, law enforcement agencies, and the general public, informants, witnesses, and public source material.

SYSTEMS EXEMPTED FROM CERTAIN PROVISIONS OF THE ACT:

The Attorney General has exempted this system from subsections (c)(3), (d), (e)(1)(2) and (3), (e)(4)(G) and (H), (e)(8) (f), (g), of the Privacy Act pursuant to 5 U.S.C. 552a (j) and (k). Rules have been promulgated in accordance with the requirements of 5 U.S.C. 553 (b), (c) and (e)

LISTING OF FIELD DIVISIONS AND LEGAL ATTACHES FOR THE FEDERAL BUREAU OF INVESTIGATION FIELD DIVISIONS: Justice/FBI-999

5th Floor, 445 Broadway, Albany, NY 12201.
POB 25186, Albuquerque, NM 87125.
POB 100560, Anchorage, AK 99510.
POB 1683, Atlanta, GA 30370.
7142 Ambassador Road, Baltimore, MD 21207.
2122 Building, Birmingham, AL 35203.
John F. Kennedy Federal Office Building, Boston, MA 02203.
111 West Huron Street, Buffalo, NY 14202.
6010 Kenley Lane, Charlotte, NC 28217.
219 S. Dearborn St., Chicago, IL 60604.
POB 1277, Cincinnati, OH 45201.
1240 E. 9th St., Cleveland, OH 44199.
POB 137, Columbia, SC 29202.
1801 W. Lamar, Dallas, TX 75202.
POB 1229, Denver, CO 80201.
POB 2118, Detroit, MI 48231.
700 E. San Antonio Ave., El Paso, TX 79901.
POB 50164, Honolulu, HI 96850.
POB 61369, Houston, TX 77208.

POB 1186, Indianapolis, IN 46206.
100 W. Capitol St., Jackson, MS 39269.
POB 8928, Jacksonville, FL 32239.
POB 2449, Kansas City, MO 64142.
POB 10368, Knoxville, TN 37919.
POB 16032, Las Vegas, NV 89101.
POB 21470, Little Rock, AR 72221-1470.
11000 Wilshire Blvd., Los Angeles, CA 90024.
POB 2467, Louisville, KY 40201.
167 N. Main St., Memphis, TN 38103.
POB 592418, Miami, FL 33159.
POB 2058, Milwaukee, WI 53201.
392 Federal Building, Minneapolis, MN 55401.
POB 2128, Mobile, AL 36652.
POB 1158, Newark, NJ 07101.
POB 2058, New Haven, CT 06521.
POB 51930, New Orleans, LA 70151.
POB 1425, New York, NY 10008.
POB 3828, Norfolk, VA 23514.
POB 54511, Oklahoma City, OK 73154.
POB 548, Omaha, NE 68101.
600 Arch St., Philadelphia, PA 19106.
201 E. Indianola, Phoenix, AZ 85012.
POB 1315, Pittsburgh, PA 15230.
POB 709, Portland, OR 97207.
POB 12325, Richmond, VA 23241.
POB 13130, Sacramento, CA 95813.
POB 7251, St. Louis, MO 63177.
125 S. State St., Salt Lake City, UT 84138.
POB 1630, San Antonio, TX 78296.
880 Front St., San Diego, CA 92188.
POB 36015, San Francisco, CA 94102.
POB BT, San Juan, PR 00936.
915 2nd Ave., Seattle, WA 98174.
POB 3646, Springfield, IL 62708.
POB 172177, Tampa, FL 33602.

Washington Field Office, Washington, DC 20535.

Federal Bureau of Investigation Academy, Quantico, VA 22135.

LEGAL ATTACHES: (Send c/o the American Embassy for the Cities indicated).

Bern, Switzerland.

Bogota, Colombia (APO, Miami 34038).

Bonn, Germany (Box 310, APO, New York 09080).

Bridgetown, Barbados (Box B, FPO, Miami 34054).

Brussels, Belgium (APO, New York 09667).

Canberra, Australia (APO, San Francisco 96404-0001).

Hong Kong, B.C.C. (FPO, San Francisco 96659-0002).

London, England (Box 2, FPO, New York 09509).

Manila, Philippines (APO, San Francisco 96528).

Mexico City, Mexico (POB 3087, Laredo, TX 78044-3087).

Montevideo, Uruguay (APO, Miami 34035).

Ottawa, Canada.

Panama City, Panama (Box E, APO, Miami 34002).

Paris, France (APO, New York 09777).

Rome, Italy (APO, New York 09794).

Tokyo, Japan (APO, San Francisco 96503).

CHAPTER 7

JUSTICE/FBI-006

Electronic Surveillance (ELSUR) Indices

This file contains information which arrives from those field offices who are involved in electronic surveillance. This activity usually takes the form of telephone wiretap although it may involve other techniques such as radio intercept.

Current technology permits the use of infrared microphones which can pick up conversations from the surface of closed window glass at some distance (for example, the 40th floor window of an adjacent office tower).

As well, it is a simple matter to intercept digital information from FAX machines and computers. It should not be overlooked that the FBI has access to the resources of a little-known government agency known as National Security Agency (NSA). NSA customarily works in collaboration with the CIA in the collection of electronic information from all over the world. They are capable of satellite intercept from virtually anywhere and possess computers capable of breaking any code known to mankind.

It is interesting to note that the FBI has asked the president to prohibit the importation or use of certain commercially available encryption devices. The equipment is used by industry to protect its trade secrets during communications. It seems the bureau is having some difficulty in its routine interception. It would be consistent, however, for the FBI to be more concerned about its own ability to monitor the public than the possible loss of American technology to foreign industrial espionage.

Then, more traditionally, there is the whole universe of "bugs", miniature radio transmitters which can be planted anywhere. In short, if the FBI really wants to eavesdrop . . . they can.

Data kept covers individuals who have been named as targets in court ordered monitoring, those who own or lease the premises covered by the surveillance, and anyone, clearly identified or not, who is overheard in such monitoring. You may find it interesting that permanent records are opened for persons overheard when only their first name is known.

The Bureau does not want the public to know much about this aspect of their investigations. In general, you will find them to be much more touchy about their "methods and techniques" than about the information they gather.

Very little is actually disclosed in this document except that the Bureau routinely monitors not only defendants, but also witnesses and attorneys. Not surprisingly, significant portions of the system are exempted from the provisions of the Privacy Act.

GOVERNMENT TEXT

JUSTICE/FBI 006

SYSTEM NAME: Electronic Surveillance (ELSUR)

SYSTEM LOCATION:

Federal Bureau of Investigation
J. Edgar Hoover Bldg.
10th and Pennsylvania Ave., NW.
Washington, DC 20535.

Those field offices which have sought conducted electronic surveillances also maintain an index. See appendix to System 022.

CATEGORIES OF INDIVIDUALS COVERED BY THE SYSTEM:

Individuals who have been the targets of direct electronic surveillance coverage by FBI in a court order; those whose communications have been monitored/intercepted by an FBI electronic surveillance installation; those who own, lease, or license premises subjected to electronic surveillance coverage sought by the FBI in a court order.

CATEGORIES OF RECORDS IN THE SYSTEM:

The ELSUR Index is comprised of three types of 3 x 5 cards:

1. Principal cards identify, by true name or best known name, all interceptees (targets) identified in an application filed by the FBI in support of an affidavit seeking a court order to conduct an electronic surveillance;
2. Proprietary Interest cards identify entities and/or individuals who own, lease, license or otherwise hold a possessory interest in locations subjected to an electronic surveillance sought by the FBI in a court order.
3. Overhear cards identify, by true name or best known name, individuals and/or entities who have been reasonably identified by a first name or initial and a last name a being a party to a communication monitored/intercepted by the FBI.

AUTHORITY FOR MAINTENANCE OF THE SYSTEM:

The ELSUR Index was initiated in October, 1966, at the recommendation of the Department of Justice and relates to electronic surveillances conducted/sought by the FBI since 1/1/60. The authority for the maintenance of these records is Title 5, Section 301, USC, which grants the Attorney General the authority to issue rules and regulations prescribing how Department of Justice information can be employed. Title 18, U.S.C., Section 3504, also sets forth recordkeeping requirements.

ROUTINE USES OF RECORDS MAINTAINED IN THE SYSTEM, INCLUDING CATEGORIES OF USERS AND THE PURPOSES OF SUCH USES:

The Elsur Indices are utilized: (1) To respond to judicial inquiries about possible electronic surveillance coverage of witnesses, defendants, or attorneys involved in Federal court proceedings, and (2) To enable the Government to certify whether a person regarding whom court-order authority is being sought for electronic coverage has ever been so covered in the past. The actual users of the indices are always employees of the FBI.

In addition, information may be released to the news media and the public pursuant to 28 CFR 50.2 unless it is determined that release of the specific information in the context of a particular case would constitute an unwarranted invasion of personal privacy;

Member of Congress or staff acting upon the member's behalf when the member or staff requests the information on behalf of and at the request of the individual who is the subject of the record; and, to the National Archives and Records Administration and the General Services Administration in records management inspections conducted under the authority of 44 U.S.C. 2904 and 2908 to the extent that legislation governing the records permits.

POLICIES AND PRACTICES FOR STORING, RETRIEVING, ACCESSING, RETAINING, AND DISPOSING OF RECORDS IN THE SYSTEM:

STORAGE:

The records are maintained manually on 3 x 5 cards.

RETRIEVABILITY:

Names/facilities are indexed and filed alphabetically. Telephone numbers and other such serial or identification numbers targeted are indexed and filed numerically. Locations targeted are indexed by address and filed by street name.

SAFEGUARDS:

The index is maintained in a restricted access room at all times. The entrance is equipped with a special locking device and alarm system for off-duty hours when the index is not in use.

RETENTION AND DISPOSAL:

Until advised to the contrary by the Department, the courts or Congress, these indices will be maintained indefinitely. The indices have been declared permanent by NARA. (Job No. NC1-65-82-4, Part E. 2. t.)

SYSTEM MANAGER(S) AND ADDRESS:

Director, Federal Bureau of Investigation,

Washington, DC 20535.

NOTIFICATION PROCEDURE:

Same as the above.

RECORD ACCESS PROCEDURES:

Inquiry addressed to Director, FBI, Washington, D.C. 20535.

CONTESTING RECORD PROCEDURES:

Same as the above.

RECORD SOURCE CATEGORIES:

Category of Individual.

SYSTEM EXEMPTED FROM CERTAIN PROVISIONS OF THE ACT:

The Attorney General has exempted this system from subsections (c) (3) and (4), (d), (e) (1), (2) and (3), (e)(4) (G) and (H), (e) (5) and (8), (f), (g) and (m) of the Privacy Act pursuant to 5 U.S.C. 552a(j). Rules have been promulgated in accordance with the requirements of 5 U.S.C. 553 (b), (c) and (e) and have been published in the Federal Register.

CHAPTER 8

JUSTICE/FBI-009
Identification (Fingerprint) Division Records System

The legendary FBI fingerprint files have come a long way since their inception. With the advent of computer scanning technology, the search procedure has become practically automatic. Although interestingly, the final match is always made manually. The file contains two types of records, criminal (nationwide) and non-criminal (government employees, military, and security clearances). In addition, tagged onto the criminal records is a ''rap sheet'', a brief history of the subject's encounters with the authorities.

The search time has come way down as well. Fingerprints can be sent by FAX or computer data lines in digital format. The inquiry is performed automatically by computer and several match candidates are retrieved for confirmation by the operator-specialist.

According to FBI policy concerning this file, a fingerprint card and the associated arrest information is destroyed if so ordered by the local agency which originated it. Other than this, the records are retained until ago 80 (75 for civil) or 7 years following the death of the subject.

This system is exempted from significant portions of the Privacy Act.

GOVERNMENT TEXT

JUSTICE/FBI-009

SYSTEM NAME: Identification Division Records System

SYSTEM LOCATION:

Federal Bureau of Investigation

J. Edgar Hoover Bldg.

10th and Pennsylvania Avenue NW

Washington, DC 20537-9700

CATEGORIES OF INDIVIDUALS COVERED BY THE SYSTEM:

A. Individuals fingerprinted as a result of arrest or incarceration.

B. Persons fingerprinted as a result of Federal employment applications, military service, alien registration and naturalization purposes and individuals desiring to have their fingerprints placed on record with the FBI for personal identification purposes.

CATEGORIES OF RECORDS IN THE SYSTEM:

A. Criminal fingerprint cards and related criminal justice information submitted by authorized agencies having criminal justice responsibilities.

B. Civil fingerprint cards submitted by Federal agencies and civil fingerprint cards submitted by persons desiring to have their fingerprints placed on record for personal identification purposes.

C. Identification records sometimes referred to as "rap sheets" which are compilations of criminal history information pertaining to individuals who have criminal fingerprint cards maintained in the system.

D. An alphabetical name index pertaining to all individuals whose fingerprints are maintained in the system.

AUTHORITY FOR MAINTENANCE OF THE SYSTEM:

The system is established, maintained and used under authority granted by 28 U.S.C. 534, 15 U.S.C. 78q. 7 U.S.C. 12a, and Pub. L. 92-544 (86 Stat. 1115), and Pub. L. 99-399. The authority is also codified in 28 CFR 0.85(b) and (j).

ROUTINE USES OF RECORDS MAINTAINED IN THE SYSTEM, INCLUDING CATEGORIES OF USERS AND THE PURPOSES OF SUCH USES:

The FBI operates the Identification Division Records System to perform identification and criminal history record information functions, for Federal, State, local, and foreign criminal justice agencies, and for noncriminal justice agencies, and other entities where authorized by Federal statute, State statue pursuant to Pub. L. {PG 49175} 92-544 (86 Stat. 1115). Presidential executive order, or regulation of the Attorney General of the United States. In addition, identification assistance is provided in disasters and for other humanitarian purposes.

Information may be released to the news media and the public pursuant to 28 CFR 20.33(a)(4), 20.33(c), and 50.2, unless it is determined that release of the specific information in the context of a particular case would constitute an unwarranted invasion of personal privacy; to a Member of Congress or staff acting upon the member's behalf when the member or staff requests the information on behalf of and at the request of the individual who is the subject of the record; and, to the National Archives and Records Administration and the General Services Administration in records management inspections conducted under the authority of 44 U.S.C. 2904 and 2906.

POLICIES AND PRACTICES FOR STORING RETRIEVING, ACCESSING, RETAINING, AND DISPOSING OF RECORDS IN THE SYSTEM:

STORAGE:

Information in the system is stored manually in file cabinets either in its natural state or on microfilm. In addition, some of the information is stored in computerized data storage devices.

RETRIEVABILITY:

(1) Information in the system is retrievable by technical fingerprint classification and positive identification is effected only by comparison of unique identifying characteristics appearing in fingerprint impressions submitted for search against the fingerprint cards maintained within the system.

(2) An auxiliary means of retrieval is through alphabetical name indexes which contain names of the individuals, their birth date, other physical descriptors, and

the individuals technical fingerprint classification and FBI numbers, if such have been assigned.

SAFEGUARDS:

Information in the system is unclassified. Disclosure of information from the system is made only to authorized recipients upon authentication and verification of the right to access the system by such persons and agencies. The physical security and maintenance of information within the system is provided by FBI rules, regulations and procedures.

RETENTION AND DISPOSAL:

(1) The Archivist of the United States has approved the destruction of records maintained in the criminal file when the records indicated individuals have reached 80 years of age, and the destruction of records maintained in the civil file when the records indicate individuals have reached 75 years of age. (Job. No. NC1-65-76-1 and NN-171-16)

(2) Fingerprint cards and related arrest data in the system are destroyed seven years following notification of the death of an individual whose records is maintained in the system. (Job No. 351-S190)

(3) Fingerprint cards submitted by State and local criminal justice agencies are removed from the system and destroyed upon the request of the submitting agencies. The destruction of a fingerprint card under this procedure results in the deletion from the system of all arrest information related to that fingerprint card.

(4) Fingerprint cards and related arrest data are removed from the Identification Division Records System upon receipt of Federal court orders for expunctions when accompanied by necessary identifying information. Recognizing lack of jurisdiction of local and State courts over an entity of the Federal Government, the Identification Division Records System, as a matter of comity, destroys fingerprint cards and related arrest data submitted by local and State criminal justice agencies upon receipt of orders of expunction directed to such agencies by local and State courts when accompanied by necessary identifying information.

SYSTEM MANAGER(S) AND ADDRESS:

Director, Federal Bureau of Investigation
10th and Pennsylvania Avenue NW
Washington, DC 20535

NOTIFICATION PROCEDURE:

Address inquiries to the System Manager.

RECORD ACCESS PROCEDURE:

The Attorney General has exempted the Identification Division Records System from compliance with subsection (d) of the Act. However, pursuant to 28 CFR 16.30-34, and Rules and Regulations promulgated by the Department of Justice on May 20, 1975 at 40 FR 22144 (Section 20.34) for Criminal Justice Information Systems, an individual is permitted access to his identification record maintained in the Identification Division Records System and procedures are furnished for correcting or challenging alleged deficiencies appearing therein.

RECORD CONTESTING PROCEDURES:

Same as above.

RECORD SOURCE CATEGORIES:

See Categories of Individuals.

SYSTEMS EXEMPTED FROM CERTAIN PROVISIONS OF THE ACT:

The Attorney General has exempted this system from subsections (c)(3) and (4); (d); (e)(1), (2), (3), (4)(G) and (H), (5) and (8); (f); and (g) of the Privacy Act pursuant to 5 U.S.C. 552a(j). Rules have been promulgated in accordance with the requirements of 5 U.S.C. 553(b), (c) and (e) and have been published in the Federal Register.

CHAPTER 9

JUSTICE/FBI-015

National Center for the Analysis of Violent Crime (NCAVC)

This system's stated purpose is to enable the Behavioral Science Unit at the FBI Academy to do research on the subject of violent crime in general. The concept is to assist all law enforcement agencies in dealing with this type of problem. An index is maintained of all detected trends, patterns, profiles, and methods of operation, both known and unknown. As well as crimes and criminals, the file also contains academic, forensic, and media articles of interest.

The troublesome aspect of this system is that it is quasi-operational as well. Beyond the normal criminal information usually found in FBI files concerning subjects and suspects, the NCAVC contains references to victims, witnesses, relatives, medical personnel, and associates. In addition it contains persons who were the subject of anonymous information or furnished information to the FBI.

It is not at all obvious why this system exists as a separate entity. It seems as though it could simply be an index to the FBI Central Files system. Nonetheless, it is not only separate, but it is maintained at the FBI's academic ivory tower at the Quantico, Virginia Training Center. It is a research aid, yet the system is fed from operational field reports from local police agencies, and is used routinely as an investigative aid for all levels of law enforcement.

Moreover, as you would expect, the system is exempt from large portions of the Privacy Act. The records access procedure requires that effectively, one must already have the record in question, in order to be able to sufficiently describe it in the access request. Additionally, if there is a proceeding either active or contemplated, access will be denied.

The rules are essentially the same as the Central Files System. If we are to believe that the system is used exclusively for dealing with the problem of violent crime, there can be no serious criticism. However, as with nearly everything we read in these documents, under the authority for dissemination, there are some topics which simply sound odd. There seems to be an inordinate amount of discussion about litigation against the FBI, the involvement of members of Congress and the press, and an inexplicable reference to the Equal Employment Opportunity Commission.

The NVACP is a new system and has not evolved into its final form. Already though, from its official description, it shows signs of being extended well beyond its original legitimate concept.

GOVERNMENT TEXT

JUSTICE/FBI-015

SYSTEM NAME: National Center for the Analysis of Violent Crime (NCAVC).

SYSTEM LOCATION:

Federal Bureau of Investigation

Training Division, FBI Academy

Behavioral Science Unit

Quantico, Virginia 22135

CATEGORIES OF INDIVIDUALS COVERED BY THE SYSTEM:

A. Individuals who relate in any manner to official FBI investigations into violent crimes including, but not limited to, subjects, suspects, victims, witnesses, close relatives, medical personnel, and associates who are relevant to an investigation.

B. Individuals who are the subject of unsolicited information or who offer unsolicited information, and law enforcement personnel who request assistance and/or make inquiries concerning records.

C. Individuals who are the subject of violent crime research studies including, but not limited to, criminal personality profiles, scholarly journals, and news media references.

CATEGORIES OF RECORDS IN THE SYSTEM:

The National Center for the Analysis of Violent Crime will maintain in both manual and automated formats, case investigation reports on all forms of solved and unsolved violent crimes. These violent crimes include, but are not limited to, acts or attempted acts of murder, kidnapping, incendiary arson or bombing, rape, physical torture, sexual trauma, or evidence of violent forms of death. Less than ten percent of the records which are analyzed may not be directly related to violent activities.

A. Violent Criminal Apprehension Program (VICAP) case reports submitted to the FBI by a duly constituted Federal, State, county, or municipal law enforcement agency in any violent criminal matter. VICAP reports include but are not limited to, crime scene descriptions, victim and offender descriptive data, laboratory reports, criminal history records, court records, news media references, crime scene photographs, and statements.

B. Violent crime case reports submitted by FBI headquarters or field offices.

C. Violent crime research studies, scholarly journal articles, textbooks, training materials, and news media references of interest to NCAVC personnel.

D. An index of all detected trends, patterns, profiles and methods of operation of known and unknown violent criminals whose records are maintained in the system.

E. An index of the names, addresses, and contact telephone numbers of professional individuals and organizations who are in a position to furnish assistance to the FBI's NCAVC operation.

F. An index of public record sources for historical, statistical and demographic data collected by the U.S. Bureau of the Census.

G. An alphabetical name index pertaining to all individuals whose records are maintained in the system.

AUTHORITY FOR MAINTENANCE OF THE SYSTEM:

44 U.S.C. Section 3101; 41 CFR Subpart 101-11.2 and 28 U.S.C. Section 534.

ROUTINE USES OF RECORDS MAINTAINED IN THE SYSTEM, INCLUDING CATEGORIES OF USERS AND THE PURPOSES OF SUCH USES:

As currently envisioned, the NCAVC will be administered by the FBI through its Training Division's Behavioral Science Unit Located at the FBI Academy, Quantico, Virginia. Its primary mission is to consolidate research, training, and operational support activities for the express purposes of providing expertise to any legitimate law enforcement agency confronted with unusual, bizarre, and/or particularly vicious or repetitive violent crimes.

Records described above are maintained in this system to permit the FBI to function efficiently as an authorized, responsive component of the Department of Justice. Therefore, the information in this system is disclosed to officials and employees of the Department of Justice, and/or all components thereof, who need the information to perform their official duties.

Information in this system may be disclosed as a routine use to any Federal, State, local, or foreign government agency directly engaged in the criminal justice process where {PG 49177} access is directly related to a law enforcement function of the recipient agency in connection with the tracking identification, and apprehension of persons believed to be engaged in repeated or exceptionally violent acts of criminal behavior.

Information in this system may be disclosed as a routine use in a proceeding before a court or adjudicative body, e.g., the Equal Employment Opportunity Commission and the Merit System Protection Board, before which the FBI is authorized to appear, when (a) the FBI or any employee thereof in his or her official capacity, or (b) any employee in his or her individual capacity where the Department of Justice has agreed to represent the employee, or (c) the United States, where the FBI determines it is likely to be affected by the litigation, is a party to litigation or has an interest in litigation and such records are determined by the FBI to be relevant to the litigation.

Information in this system may be disclosed as a routine use to an organization or individual in both the public or private sector pursuant to an appropriate legal proceeding or, if deemed necessary, to elicit information or cooperation from the recipient for use by the FBI in the performance of an authorized activity. An example could be where the activities of an individual are disclosed to a member of the public to elicit his/her assistance in FBI apprehension or detection efforts.

Information in this system may be disclosed as a routine use to an organization or individual in the public or private sector where there is reason to believe the recipient is or could become the target of a particular criminal activity or conspiracy and to the extent the information is relevant to the protection of life or property.

Relevant information may be disclosed from this system to the news media and general public where there exists a legitimate public interest. Examples would include: to obtain public or media assistance in the tracking, identifying, and apprehending of persons believed to be engaged in repeated acts of violent criminal behavior; to notify the public and/or media of arrests; to protect the public from imminent threat to life or property where necessary; and to disseminate information to the public and/or media to obtain cooperation with violent crime research, evaluation, and statistical programs.

Information in this system may be disclosed as is necessary to appropriately respond to congressional inquiries on behalf of constituents.

A record from a system of records may be disclosed as a routine use to the National Archives and Records Administration (NARA) in records management inspections conducted under the authority of 44 U.S.C. 2904 and 2906 to the extent that legislation governing the record permits.

POLICIES AND PRACTICES FOR STORING, RETRIEVING, ACCESSING, RETAINING, AND DISPOSING OF RECORDS IN THE SYSTEM:

STORAGE:

Information in the system is stored manually in locked file cabinets, either in its natural state or on microfilm, at the NCAVC in Quantico, Virginia. The active main files are maintained in hard copy form and some inactive records are maintained on microfilm.

In addition, some of the information is stored in computerized data storage devices at the NCAVC and FBI Computer Center in Washington, DC. Investigative information which is maintained in computerized form may be stored in memory on disk storage on computer tape, or on computer printed listings.

RETRIEVABILITY:

On-line computer access to NCAVC files is achieved by using the following search descriptors:

A. A data base which contains the names of individuals, their birth dates, physical descriptions, and other identification numbers such as FBI numbers, if such have been assigned.

B. Summary variables contained on VICAP reports submitted to the NCAVC as previously described.

C. Key words citations to violent crime research studies, scholarly journal articles, textbooks, training materials, and media references.

SAFEGUARDS:

Records are maintained in restricted areas and accessed only by FBI employees. All FBI employees receive a complete pre-employment background investigation. All employees are cautioned about divulging confidential information or any information contained in FBI files. Failure to abide by this provision violates Department of Justice regulations and may violate certain statutes providing maximum severe penalties of a ten thousand dollar fine or 10 years' imprisonment or both. Employees who resign or retire are also cautioned about divulging information acquired in the job.

Registered mail is used to transmit routine hard copy records between field offices. Highly classified records are hand carried by Special Agents or personnel of the Armed Forces Courier Service. Highly classified or sensitive privacy information, which is electronically transmitted between field offices and to and from FBI Headquarters, is transmitted in encrypted form to prevent interception and interpretation.

Information transmitted in teletype form between the NCAVC in Quantico, Virginia and the FBI Computer Center in Washington, DC, is encrypted prior to transmission at both places to ensure confidentiality and security of the data.

FBI field offices involved in certain complicated, investigative matters may be provided with on-line access to the computerized information which is maintained for them on disc storage in the FBI Computer Center in Washington, DC. This computerized data is also transmitted in encrypted form.

RETENTION AND DISPOSAL:

Records are proposed for destruction after 50 years or upon termination of the program, whichever is earlier. The dispo-sition schedule is pending with NARA as Job No. N1-65-88- 13.

SYSTEM MANAGER(S) AND ADDRESS:

Director, Federal Bureau of Investigation
10th and Pennsylvania Avenue, NW
Washington, DC 20535

NOTIFICATION PROCEDURE:

Address inquiries to the System Manager.

RECORDS ACCESS PROCEDURES:

Requests for access to records in this system shall be made in writing with the envelope and the letter clearly marked "Privacy Access Request". The request must provide the full name, complete address, date of birth, place of birth, and notarized signature of the individual who is the subject of the record requested. The request should also include the general subject matter of the document or its file number-along with any other known information which may assist in making a search of the records. The request must also provide a return addressing for transmitting the information. Access requests should be addressed to the Director, Federal Bureau of Investigation, Washington, D.C. 20535.

RECORD CONTESTING PROCEDURE:

Individuals desiring to contest or amend information maintained in the system should also direct their request to the Director, Federal Bureau of Investigation, Washington, D.C. 20535. The request should state clearly and concisely (1) the reasons for contesting the information, and (2) the proposed amendment to the information. {PG 49178}

RECORD SOURCE CATEGORIES:

The FBI, by the very nature of its responsibilities to investigate violations of law within its investigative jurisdiction and ensure the internal security of the United States, collects information from a wide variety of sources. Basically, information is obtained, as a result of investigative efforts, from other Government agencies, law enforcement agencies, the general public, informants, witnesses, and public source material.

SYSTEM EXEMPTED FROM CERTAIN PROVISIONS OF THE ACT:

The Attorney General has exempted this system from subsections (c)(3), (d), (e)(1), (e)(4)(G) and (H), (f) and (g) of the Privacy Act pursuant to 5 U.S.C. 552a (j)(2) and (k)(2). Rules have been promulgated in accordance with the requirements of 5 U.S.C. 553 (b), (c), and (e).

CHAPTER 10

JUSTICE/INS-008

Bond Accounting and Control System

This file, maintained in cooperation with the Immigration and Naturalization Service, covers any individuals who have posted a bond with the INS, and the beneficiaries (aliens). It is used by a variety of agencies to perform routine accounting functions on bond matters, statistical analysis, as well as to monitor the collection of breached bonds.

The system is fully covered by the Privacy Act, but with one sticky exception. The Privacy Act does not benefit aliens who have not yet been granted permanent legal residence in the U.S. It would be a fair assumption to say that this effectively excludes most persons in the file from having access.

It seems harmless enough with its purely administrative function . . . until you ask "What is an immigration bond?"

It never occurs to most American citizens that their government requires a substantial security deposit to be submitted along with immigration applications, simply to guarantee that applicants remain visible. This is a policy which not widely imposed around the world. But, it is consistent with the American government's attitude of "trust no one". More commonly, countries require a "referee", that is, a citizen of stature, such as a doctor or attorney, to vouch for an alien. But, bonds are an American phenomenon.

This entire system, and those who man it would make a good candidate for the list of "public services" we could easily do without when it comes time to do some serious budget cutting.

GOVERNMENT TEXT

JUSTICE/INS-008

SYSTEM NAME: Bond Accounting and Control System (BACS).

SYSTEM LOCATIONS:

Immigration and Naturalization Service regional offices:

(1) Burlington, Vermont

(2) Fort Snelling, Twin Cities, Minnesota

(3) Dallas, Texas

(4) Laguna Niguel, California

Addresses of offices are listed in JUSTICE/INS-999 as published in the Federal Register, or in the telephone directories of the respective cities listed above under the heading "United States Government, Immigration and Naturalization Service."

CATEGORIES OF INDIVIDUALS COVERED BY THE SYSTEM:

Individuals who have posted a bond with INS and the beneficiaries of posted bonds.

CATEGORIES OF RECORDS IN THE SYSTEM:

Information which allows identification of active bonds posted with INS such as: bond number, obligor's name and address, alien beneficiary's name and alien file number, type of bond, location and date bond was posted, and other data related to bonds.

AUTHORITY FOR MAINTENANCE OF THE SYSTEM:

Section 103 (8 U.S.C. 1103) in implementing the authorities set forth in Section 213 (8 U.S.C. 1183) and Section 293 (8 U.S.C. 1353) of the Immigration and Nationality Act.

PURPOSE(S):

Information in this system will be used by employees of INS to control and account for collateral received to support an immigration bond. The system will allow prompt location of related files and other records and will enable INS to make timely responses to inquiries about these records.

The information in the system can be used to generate various documents (such as voucher disbursements) required for normal accounting procedures and to generate statistical and historical reports pertaining to immigration bonds posted, cancelled or breached.

ROUTINE USES OF RECORDS MAINTAINED IN THE SYSTEM, INCLUDING CATEGORIES OF USERS AND THE PURPOSES OF SUCH USES:

Relevant information contained in this system of records may be disclosed as follows:

A. To other Federal, state, or local law enforcement agencies for investigative purposes or collection of breached bonds.

B. To a member of Congress or staff upon the member's behalf when the member or staff acting requests the information on behalf of and at the request of the individual who is the subject of the record.

C. To the National Archives and Records Administration and the General Services Administration in records management inspections conducted under the authority of 44 U.S.C. 2904 and 2906.

POLICIES AND PRACTICES FOR STORING, RETRIEVING, ACCESSING, RETAINING, AND DISPOSING OF RECORDS IN THE SYSTEM:

STORAGE:

Information is stored on magnetic disks.

RETRIEVABILITY:

Records may be retrieved by any of the following: Alien's name, alien's file number, obligor's name, bond-receipt control number, breach control number, or location and date bond was posted.

SAFEGUARDS:

Records are safeguarded in accordance with Department of Justice rules and procedures. INS offices are located in buildings under security guard, and access to premises is by official identification. All records are stored in spaces which are locked outside of normal office hours. Access to this automated system is obtained through remote terminals which are located in secured areas and require the use of restricted passwords.

RETENTION AND DISPOSAL:

Records are deleted from magnetic disks one year (or earlier) after the bond is disbursed and the file closed.

SYSTEM MANAGER(S) AND ADDRESS:

The Associate Regional Commissioner, management, at the regional office having jurisdiction over the area in which the beneficiary alien resides. See the caption "System locations."

NOTIFICATION PROCEDURES:

Inquiries should be addressed to the system manager.

RECORD ACCESS PROCEDURE:

In all cases, requests for access to a record shall be in writing. Written requests may be submitted by mail or in person at an INS office. If a request for access is made by mail, the envelope and letter shall be clearly marked "Privacy Access Request." To identify a record relating to an individual, a requester should provide: The individual's full name, alien file number, and location and date bond was posted. The requester shall provide a return address for transmitting the information.

CONTESTING RECORD PROCEDURES:

Any individual desiring to contest or amend information maintained in the system should direct his request to the regional INS office in which he believes the record concerning him may exist. The request should state clearly what information is being contested, the reasons for contesting it, and the proposed amendment to the information.

RECORD SOURCE CATEGORIES:

Information contained in this system or records is supplied on INS forms by individuals who have posted a bond with the INS and by the beneficiaries of posted bonds.

SYSTEMS EXEMPTED FROM CERTAIN PROVISIONS OF THE ACT: None.

CHAPTER 11

JUSTICE/INS-009
Alien Status Verification Index

This system is also maintained in cooperation with the INS. It is a master file of all known aliens, those which have immigration applications or petitions in any stage of processing, and those who are known to be illegal. The system is nationwide and in addition to INS locations, there are terminals in State Employment Security (welfare) offices and other selected local offices.

The system is used to verify an alien's immigration status for whatever purpose. Security for remote terminals is accomplished by password and physical security. The system is covered by the Privacy Act without exception. This of course, means that only legal permanent US residents may see or contest their files.

This file is of no real concern to American citizens. However, if you happen to be of other than U.S. nationality and are in the United States for any reason, you have good reason to be concerned about it. In addition to the questionable function of purging the country of "undesirable aliens", a category which has mainly to do with paperwork, not a potential threat to society, the system is used as an apparatus to monitor all foreigners. Any agency of the government, or any private entity may file a report which can trigger a file to be opened, then subsequent observation as a suspected undesirable alien.

The list of things which can cause your file to be initialized is immense. It could be a large bank transaction, publication of an article critical of the government, applying for a visa to travel to a country in disfavor with the United States, or merely talking to someone who, unbeknown to you, is under investigation.

Further to this, at some point, there is the risk of your record being fed to the "watch file". Then upon your next entry into the U.S., you could be detained for questioning, or even denied entry. There is no recourse.

GOVERNMENT TEXT

JUSTICE/INS-009

SYSTEM NAME: Alien Status Verification Index

SYSTEM LOCATION:

Central, Regional, District, and other files control offices of the Immigration and Nationalization Service (INS) in the United States as detailed in JUSTICE/INS-999.

Remote access terminals will also be located in state employment security offices (SESA's) and other Federal, State, and local agencies nationwide.

CATEGORIES OF INDIVIDUALS COVERED BY THE SYSTEM:

Individuals covered by provisions of the immigration and nationality laws of the United States.

CATEGORIES OF RECORDS IN THE SYSTEM:

The system consists of an index of aliens and other persons on whom INS has a record as an applicant, petitioner, beneficiary, or possible violator of the Immigration and Nationality Act. Records are limited to index and file locator data including name, alien registration number (or "A-file" number), date and place of birth, social security account number, date, coded {PG 49181} status transaction data and immigration status classification.

AUTHORITY FOR MAINTENANCE OF THE SYSTEM:

Section 290, of the Immigration and Nationality Act, as amended (8 U.S.C. 1360).

PURPOSE:

This system of records is used to verify an alien's immigration status.

ROUTINE USES OF RECORDS MAINTAINED IN THE SYSTEM, INCLUDING CATEGORIES OF USERS AND THE PURPOSES OF SUCH USES:

Relevant information contained in this system of records may be disclosed as follows:

A. To a Federal, State, or local government agency, in response to its request in connection with the hiring or retention of an employee, the issuance of a security clearance, the reporting of an investigation of an employee, the letting of a contract, or the issuance of a license, grant, or other benefit by the requesting agency, to the extent that the information is relevant and necessary to the requesting agency's decision on the matter.

B. To other Federal, State, or local government agencies for the purpose of verifying information in conjunction with the conduct of a national intelligence and security investigation or for criminal or civil law enforcement purposes.

C. To the news media and the public pursuant to 28 CFR 50.2 unless it is determined that release of the specific information in the context of a particular case would constitute an unwarranted invasion of personal privacy.

D. To a Member of Congress or staff acting upon the Member's behalf when the Member of staff request the information on behalf of and at the request of the individual who is the subject of the record.

E. To the National Archives and Records Administration and the General Services Administration in records management inspections conducted under the authority of 44 U.S.C. 2904 and 2906.

POLICIES AND PRACTICES FOR STORING, RETRIEVING, ACCESSING, RETAINING, AND DISPOSING OF RECORDS IN THE SYSTEM:

STORAGE:

Records are stored on magnetic disk and tape.

RETRIEVABILITY:

Records are indexed and retrievable by name and date and place of birth, or by name and social security account number, by name and A-file number.

SAFEGUARDS:

Records are safeguarded in accordance with Department of Justice rules and procedures. Access is controlled by restricted password for use of remote terminals in secured areas.

RETENTION AND DISPOSAL:

Centralized index records stored on magnetic disk and tape are updated periodically and maintained for the life of the related record.

SYSTEM MANAGER AND ADDRESS:

The Associate Commissioner, Information Systems
Immigration and Naturalization Service
Central Office, 425 I Street NW
Washington, D.C.

is the sole manager of the system.

NOTIFICATION PROCEDURE:

Inquiries should be addressed to the system manager listed above.

RECORD ACCESS PROCEDURES:

In all cases, requests for access to a record from this system shall be in writing. If a request for access is made by mail the envelope and letter shall be clearly marked "Privacy Act Request." The requester shall include the name, date and place of birth of the person whose record is sought and if known, the alien file number. The requester shall also provide a return address for transmitting the information.

RECORD CONTESTING PROCEDURES:

Any individual desiring to contest or amend information maintained in the system should direct has request to the System Manager or to the INS office that maintains the life. The request should state clearly what information is being contested, the reasons for contesting it, and the proposed amendment to the information.

RECORD SOURCE CATEGORIES:

Basic information contained in this system is taken from Department of State and INS applications and reports on the individual.

SYSTEMS EXEMPTED FROM CERTAIN PROVISIONS OF THE ACT: None.

CHAPTER 12

JUSTICE/INS-012
Deportable Alien Control System (DACS)

The DAC system provides INS with an automated database which assists in the arrest, deportation, or detention of aliens in accordance with immigration and nationality laws. It also services as a docket and control system by providing management with information concerning the status and/or disposition of deportable aliens. The system is managed by the INS Commissioner of Deportation and Detention in Washington, D.C.

Although it is covered under the provisions of the Privacy Act, exclusions are effected by either the "landed immigrant" requirement or the law enforcement clause, or both.

Once landed in this file system, a foreigner is pretty well finished. The United States is a veritable mine field of traps, any one of which could detect a person in this file. Although is does take a court order to deport, entry into the system usually begins with an allegation. (That is, unless the subject does something so serious that he is actually arrested). From there, an investigation ensues and legal process is prosecuted.

To the foreigner who actually believes that he can challenge the deportation, win, and walk away to live a normal life . . . think again. Once ANYONE, foreigner or citizen, comes to the notice of the "system", they are a harassed for the rest of their lives. Friendly advice . . . Barring extreme circumstances in the country of origin, leave the United States voluntarily without going through the deportation procedure. There are numerous other countries whose governments are less invasive.

GOVERNMENT TEXT

JUSTICE/INS-012

SYSTEM NAME: Deportable Alien Control System (DACS)

SYSTEM LOCATION:

Central, Regional, District, and other offices of the Immigration and Naturalization Service (INS) in the United States as detailed in JUSTICE/INS-999

CATEGORIES OF INDIVIDUALS COVERED BY THE SYSTEM:

Aliens alleged to be deportable by INS.

CATEGORIES OF RECORDS IN THE SYSTEM:

The system is a computer data base that contains biographic information about deportable aliens such as:

* Name, date and country of birth;
* United States and foreign addresses;
* File number,
* Charge,
* Amount of bond,
* Hearing date,
* Case assignment, scheduling date,
* Section(s) of law under which deportability/excludability is alleged;
* Data collected to support the INS position on deportability/excludability, including information on any criminal or subversive activities;
* Date, place, and type of last entry into the United States;
* Attorney/representative's identification number;
* Family data, and other case-related information.

AUTHORITY FOR MAINTENANCE OF THE SYSTEM:

8 U.S.C. 1103, 1251, and 1252.

PURPOSE(S):

The system provides INS with an automated data base which assists in the arrest, deportation, or detention of aliens in accordance with immigration and nationality laws. It also serves as a docket and control system by providing management with information concerning the status and/or disposition of deportable aliens.

ROUTINE USES OF RECORDS MAINTAINED IN THE SYSTEM INCLUDING CATEGORIES OF USERS AND PURPOSES OF SUCH USES:

Relevant information contained in this system of records may be disclosed as follows:

A. To clerks and judges of Federal courts exercising jurisdiction over the deportable aliens in determining grounds for deportation.

B. To other Federal, State, and local government law enforcement and regulatory agencies and foreign governments, including the Department of Defense and all components thereof, the Department of State, the Department of Treasury, the Central Intelligence Agency, the Selective Service System, the United States Coast Guard, the United Nations, and INTERPOL, and individuals and organizations during the course of investigation in the processing of a matter or during a proceeding within the purview of the immigration and nationality laws to elicit information required by INS to carry out its functions and statutory mandates.

C. Where there is an indication of a violation or potential violation of law (whether civil, criminal or regulatory in nature), {PG 49182} to the appropriate agency (whether Federal, State, local or foreign), charged with the responsibility of investigating or prosecuting such violations, or charged with enforcing or implementing the statute, rule, regulation or order issued pursuant thereto.

D. Where there is an indication of a violation or potential violation of the immigration and nationality laws, or of a general statute within INS jurisdiction or of a regulation, rule, or order issued pursuant thereto, to a court, magistrate, or administrative tribunal in the course of presenting evidence, and to opposing counsel during discovery.

E. Where there is an indication of a violation or potential violation of the law of another nation (whether civil or criminal), to the appropriate foreign government agency charged with enforcing or implementing such laws and to international organizations engaged in the collection and dissemination of intelligence concerning criminal activity.

F. To other Federal agencies for the purpose of conducting national intelligence and security investigations.

G. To a Member of Congress or staff acting on the Member's behalf when the Member or staff requests the information on behalf of and at the request of the individual who is the subject of the record.

H. To the General Services Administration and the National Archives and Records Administration in records management inspections conducted under the authority of 44 U.S.C. 2904 and 2906.

POLICIES AND PRACTICES FOR STORING, RETRIEVING ACCESSING, RETAINING, AND DISPOSING OF RECORDS IN THE SYSTEM:

STORAGE:

These records are stored in a data base on magnetic disks.

RETRIEVABILITY:

These records are retrieved by name and/or date of birth, A-file number, or by alien's Bureau of Prisons number, when applicable.

SAFEGUARDS:

INS offices are located in buildings under security guard, and access to premises is by official identification. Access to terminals is limited to INS employees with user identification numbers. Access to records in this system is by restricted password and is further protected by secondary passwords.

RETENTION AND DISPOSAL:

Deportable alien case control and detention records are marked closed and retained for statistical purposes through the end of the fiscal year. Closed cases are archived and stored in the database separate from the active cases. A retention and disposition schedule for the case summary and detention history records is currently being negotiated and will be submitted to the Archivist of the United States for approval.

SYSTEM MANAGER AND ADDRESS:

Assistant Commissioner, Detention and Deportation
Immigration and Naturalization Service
425 I Street, NW
Washington, DC 20536

NOTIFICATION PROCEDURE:

Address inquiries to the system manager identified above.

RECORDS ACCESS PROCEDURE:

Make all requests for access in writing to the Freedom of Information Act/Privacy Act (FOIA/PA) Officer at the nearest INS Office, or the INS office maintaining the desired records (if known) by using the list of Principal Offices of the Immigration and Naturalization Service Appendix, JUSTICE/INS-999, published in the Federal Register. Clearly mark the envelope and letter "Privacy Act Request." Provide the A-file number and/or the full name and date of birth, with a notarized signature of the individual who is the subject of the record, and a return address.

RECORD CONTESTING PROCEDURES:

Direct all requests to contest or amend information in the record to the FOIA/PA Officer at one of the addresses identified above. State clearly and concisely the information being contested, the reason for contesting it, and the proposed amendment thereof. Clearly mark the envelope "Privacy Act Request." The record must be identified in the same manner as described for making a request for access.

RECORD SOURCE CATEGORIES:

Basic information is obtained from "The Immigration and Naturalization Service (INS) Alien File (A File) and Central Index System, (CIS), JUSTICE/INS-001A." Information may also come from the alien, the alien's attorney/representative, INS officials, other Federal, State, local, and foreign agencies and the courts.

SYSTEMS EXEMPTED FROM CERTAIN PROVISIONS OF THE ACT: None.

CHAPTER 13

JUSTICE/DEA/INS-111

Automated Intelligence Records System (Pathfinder)

Pathfinder is a joint effort of the Drug Enforcement Agency, Immigration and Naturalization Service, and the FBI. This is a major system and is designed to manage law enforcement in the general category of illegal border traffic. This includes, drugs, money, aliens, fraudulent documents, terrorism, crewman desertions and stowaways, and arranged marriages.

In addition, the file contains individuals whose identity documents have been lost or stolen, those who arrive in the United States by private aircraft, as well as informants, witnesses and non-implicated persons with knowledge of relevant cases. The system may also contain information of any type whatsoever which is developed in the course of investigations.

As a miniature version of the FBI Central Files system, this general toolkit for border operations is fed data from:

DEA: Investigation and Intelligence Reports,

INS: Air and Marine Offices,
Operational Activities Special Information System Fraudulent Document Center,
Terrorist Index,
Reports of Investigation and Apprehension and
Coast Guard files.

In addition, data is obtained from filed flight plan information concerning individuals known, suspected or alleged to be involved in criminal smuggling activities using private aircraft. The close scrutiny of private aircraft traffic is particularly troubling. It is possible to come under suspicion for merely arriving at a border airport by private plane . . . especially if it is frequently. Similar surveillance is maintained over private marine traffic on all coasts.

This system is a good example of the networking that is beginning to take place between the various law enforcement agencies. For serious criminals, this is really bad news. And, because a well-honed blade will indiscriminately cut anyone who touches it, this can also be bad news for innocent citizens caught in the web of the justice system. The tendency is to arrest when in doubt and let the "system" sort it out.

This is very unfortunate in that, the judicial system is no longer set up to assure the rights of the accused. It is operates now to break the accused, so that he will agree to a plea bargain, giving up his right to a trial. It is an efficient system. It grinds up thousands of people each day, both criminal and innocent, keeping accurate computer records of their plight as they are sucked under one by one, into the bowels of the penal system. Defense is no longer possible in the "New World Order".

Not surprisingly, this system is exempted from virtually all of The Privacy Act . . . other than the knowledge of its existence.

GOVERNMENT TEXT

JUSTICE/DEA-INS-111

SYSTEM NAME: Automated Intelligence Records System (Pathfinder)

SYSTEM LOCATION:

U.S. Department of Justice

Drug Enforcement Administration

1405 I Street, NW

Washington, D.C. 20537

and

El Paso Intelligence Center (EPIC)

El Paso, Texas 79902.

CATEGORIES OF INDIVIDUALS COVERED BY THE SYSTEM:

(1) Those individuals who are known, suspected, or alleged to be involved in:

(a) narcotic trafficking,

(b) narcotic-arms trafficking,

(c) alien smuggling or transporting,

(d) illegally procuring, using, selling, counterfeiting, reproducing, or altering identification documents relating to status under the immigration and nationality laws,

(e) terrorist activities (narcotic, arms or alien trafficking/smuggling related),

(f) crewman desertions and stowaways,

(g) arranging or contracting a marriage to defraud the immigration laws; and

(h) facilitating the transportation of narcotics proceeds.

(2) In addition to the categories of individuals listed above, those individuals who:

(a) have had citizenship or alien identification documents put to fraudulent use or have reported them as lost or stolen,

(b) arrive in the United States from a foreign territory by private aircraft, and

(c) are informants or witnesses (including non-implicated persons) who have pertinent knowledge of some circumstances or aspect of a case or suspect may be the subject of a file within this system.

(3) In the course of criminal investigation and intelligence gathering, DEA and INS may detect violation of non-drug or non-alien related laws. In the interests of effective law enforcement, this information is retained in order to establish patterns of criminal activity and to assist other law enforcement agencies that are charged with enforcing other segments of criminal law. Therefore, under certain limited circumstances, individuals known, suspected, or alleged to be involved in non-narcotic or non-alien criminal activity may be the subject of a file maintained within this system.

CATEGORIES OF RECORDS IN THE SYSTEM:

In general, this system contains computerized and manual intelligence information gathered from DEA and INS investigative records and reports. Specifically, intelligence information is gathered and collated from the following DEA and INS records and reports;

(1) DEA Reports of Investigation (DEA-6), {PG 49183}

(2) DEA and INS Intelligence Reports,

(3) INS Air Detail Office Index (I-92A).

(4) INS Operational Activities Special Information System (OASIS).

(5) INS Marine Intelligence Index,

(6) INS Fraudulent Document Center Index,

(7) INS Terrorist Index,

(8) INS Reports of Investigation and Apprehension (I-44, I- 213, G-166)

(9) U.S. Coast Guard Vessel 408 file.

In addition, data is obtained from commercially available flight plan information concerning individuals known, suspected or alleged to be involved in criminal smuggling activities using private aircraft.

AUTHORITY FOR MAINTENANCE OF THE SYSTEM:

This system has been established in order for DEA and INS to carry out their law enforcement, regulatory, and intelligence functions mandated by The Comprehensive Drug Abuse Prevention and Control Act of 1970 (84 Stat. 1236), Reorganization Plan No. 2 of 1973, the

Single Convention on Narcotic Drugs, (18 UST 1407), and Sections 103.265, and 290 and Title III of the Immigration and Nationality Act, as amended (8 U.S.C. 1103, 1305, 1360, 1401 et seq.).

Additional authority is derived from Treaties, Statutes, Executive Orders and Presidential Proclamations which DEA and INS have been charged with administering.

ROUTINE USES OF RECORDS MAINTAINED IN THE SYSTEM INCLUDING CATEGORIES OF USERS AND THE PURPOSES OF SUCH USES:

This system will be used to produce association and link analysis reports and such special reports as required by intelligence analysts of DEA and INS. The system will also be used to provide "real-time" responses to queries from Federal, state, and local agencies charged with border law enforcement responsibilities.

Information from this system will be provided to the following categories of users for law enforcement and intelligence purposes provided a legitimate and lawful "need to know" is demonstrated:

(a) Other Federal law enforcement agencies,

(b) State and local law enforcement agencies,

(c) Foreign law enforcement agencies with whom DEA and INS maintain liaison

(d) U.S. intelligence and military intelligence agencies involved in border criminal law enforcement,

(e) Clerks and judges of courts exercising appropriate jurisdiction over subject matter maintained within this system

(f) Department of State

(g) Various Federal, State, and local enforcement committees and working groups including Congress and senior Administration officials

(h) The Department of Defense and military departments;

(i) The United Nations

(j) The International Police Organization (Interpol)

(k) To individuals and organizations in the course of investigations to elicit information; (1) to the Office of Management and Budget, upon request, in order to justify the allocation of resources;

(m) To respondents and their attorneys for purposes of discovery, formal and informal, in the course of an adjudicatory, rulemaking, or other hearing held pursuant to the Controlled Substances Act of 1970; and

(n) In the event there is an indication of a violation or potential violation of law whether civil, criminal, regulatory, or administrative in nature, the relevant information may be referred to the appropriate agency, whether Federal, state, local or foreign, charged with the responsibility of investigating or prosecuting such violation or charged with enforcing or implementing the statute or rule, regulations, or order issued pursuant thereto.

Release of information to the National Archives and Records Administration (NARA) and to the General Services Administration (GSA): A record from a system of records may be disclosed as a routine use to the NARA and GSA records management inspections conducted under the authority of 44 U.S.C. 2904 and 2906.

POLICIES AND PRACTICES FOR STORING, RETRIEVING, ACCESSING, RETAINING, AND DISPOSING OF RECORDS IN THE SYSTEM:

STORAGE:

Manual subsets of the Pathfinder Information System are maintained on standard index cards and manual folders. Standard security formats are employed. The records are stored on computer at the DOJ computer center, Washington, D.C.

RETRIEVABILITY:

Access to individual records can be accomplished by reference to either the manual indices or the automated information system. Access is achieved by reference to personal identifiers, other data elements or any combination thereof.

SAFEGUARDS:

The Pathfinder System of Records is protected by both physical security methods and dissemination and access controls. Fundamental in all cases is that access to intelligence information is limited to those persons or agencies with a demonstrated and lawful need to know for the information in order to perform assigned functions.

Physical security when intelligence files are attended is provided by responsible DEA and INS employees. Physical security when files are unattended is provided by the secure locking of material in approved containers or facilities. The selection of containers or facilities is made in consideration of the sensitivity or National Security Classification as appropriate, of the files, and the extent of security guard and/or surveillance afforded by electronic means.

Protection of the automated information system is provided by physical, procedural, and electronic means. The master file resides in the DEA Office of Intelligence Secured Computer System and is physically attended or safe-guarded on a full time basis. Access or observation to active telecommunications terminals is limited to those with a demonstrated need to know for retrieval information. Surreptitious access to an unattended terminal is precluded by a complex authentication procedure. The procedure is provided only to authorized DEA and INS employees. Transmission from DEA Headquarters to El Paso, Texas is accomplished via a dedicated secured line.

An automated log of queries is maintained for each terminal. Improper procedure results in no access and under certain conditions completely locks out the terminal pending restoration by the master controller at DEA Headquarters after appropriate verification. Unattended terminals are otherwise located in locked facilities after normal working hours.

The dissemination of intelligence information to an individual outside the Department of Justice is made in accordance with the routine uses as described herein and otherwise in accordance with conditions of disclosure prescribed in the Privacy Act. The need to know is determined in both cases by DEA and INS as a prerequisite to the release of information.

RETENTION AND DISPOSAL:

Records maintained within this system are retained for fifty-five (55) years.

SYSTEM MANAGERS AND ADDRESSES:

Deputy Assistant Administrator, Office of Intelligence Drug Enforcement Administration

1405 I Street, NW

Washington, D.C. 20537

and

Associate Commissioner, Enforcement
Immigration and Naturalization Service
425 I Street, NW
Washington, D.C. 20536

NOTIFICATION PROCEDURE:

Inquiries should be addressed to:

Freedom of Information Section
Drug Enforcement Administration
1405 I Street, NW
Washington, D.C. 20537

RECORD ACCESS PROCEDURE:

Same as notification procedure.

CONTESTING RECORD PROCEDURES:

Same as notification procedure.

RECORD SOURCE CATEGORIES:

- Commercially available flight plan information source;
- Confidential informants;
- DEA intelligence and investigative records/reports;
- INS investigative, intelligence and statutory mandated records/reports;
- Records/reports of other Federal, state and local agencies;
- Records/reports of foreign agencies with whom DEA maintains liaison.

SYSTEMS EXEMPTED FROM CERTAIN PROVISIONS OF THE ACT:

The Attorney General has exempted this system from subsections (c) (3) and (4), (d), (e), (1), (2), and (3), (e)(4)(g), (H) and (I), (e) (5) and (8), (f), (g), and (h) of the Privacy Act pursuant to 5 U.S.C. 552a(j) and(k). Rules have been promulgated in accordance with the requirements of 5 U.S.C. 553(b), (c) and (e) and have been published in the Federal Register.

CONCLUSION

These enormous systems are by no means the whole story. Virtually every government agency maintains extensive files on the public, each oriented to their own particular specialty. For years they were only semi-automated and more or less independent. Now, as the technology and software comes of age, they are increasingly able to network the databases. When you include the Social Security Administration, we can have a degree of assurance that the FBI will soon get its wish for a dossier on everyone.

Until recently, the sheer expense and effort required, prevented the integration of the databases and minimized the danger of abuse. Now, technology has made it both cost-effective and very tempting indeed to go this last step. Concerns have been raised but, those who would benefit from system integration are also those in a position to make the decision.

And truly, from the viewpoint of administration and law enforcement, how better could they keep track of "their" public? And at what expense! George Orwell's "1984" may have missed on his prediction of a government framework, but he was deadly accurate on their technology and motivations.

The FBI now faces the challenge and also the opportunity to rise to the call of greater public responsibility. It has already gone too far in its pursuit of monitoring citizens. But it is Congress who is really to blame for creating the monster; and of course, the life work of one man, J. Edgar Hoover, for making it into an empire . . . with the full blessing of the administrations of the time.

How do you undo an information system of this extent and sophistication? . . . when 1) The people who created it regard it as a work of art and love working with it, 2) It performs very efficiently, many necessary functions of law enforcement, and 3) the FBI by law, protects the authority which created it . . . Congress.

Answer: You don't. It will never diminish . . . only grow. The solution if there is one, is old-fashioned restraint . . . responsibility, a renewed respect for the common citizen, and the repeal of a quagmire of unnecessary legislation. This would take a veritable revolution in Congress in terms of their present-day priorities and agenda.

In the FBI at all levels, and in all law enforcement agencies for that matter, there is a need for a fundamental change in the attitude of automatic suspicion. That a "citizen" in contrast to a "suspect", is just someone who has not yet been caught in an illegal act. There exists a presumption that eventually, everyone will break some law and need to be placed under the supervision of the government.

As was mentioned in the introduction, the general distrust of the public by law enforcement and government officials in general, becomes a self fulfilling prophesy. If treated in this manner long enough, the public WILL become unreliable in terms of compliance with much of legislation. As a matter of history, there is an increasing chance a country will eventually become virtually ungovernable, as we have seen in recent years in eastern Europe.

With respect to the Federal government, but especially the FBI, there is a need for an abatement in the insatiable appetite for information, much of which is collected only because "it may be needed some day." . . . needed because ultimately everyone is suspect.

Many believe that FBI personnel consider themselves "above the law". But, mention this to any official and watch them bristle. And in all fairness, they by and large, do work within the restrictions of the law. However, the "law" is in fact, the problem. A symposium of social scientists some years ago estimated that of the legislated and case law accumulated over the last century in the United States, upwards of 70% serves no material purpose.

Think of the astronomical sums of money which could be saved if a really serious chunk of legislation and the agencies which exist to serve it, simply ceased to exist. The size of government, its structures, numbers of people employed, costs, and yes . . . enforcement activities, are a direct function of legislation. The current annual combined Federal, State, and local government budgets total roughly two trillion dollars.

What would happen if half the aggregate amount (about 50,000 dollars a year for every family) were to be diverted back into the private sector to revitalize a badly mauled economy . . . to put the "private" back into private enterprise . . . to put the "rights" back into civil rights . . . and to restore the dignity that Americans have lost?

A big assist would come from the decentralization of government. The State's Rights Movement should be given the opportunity to flourish in order to give rebirth to the diversity in American culture. It was the country's numerous ethnic and cultural factions which originally fostered regional pride and the legendary work ethic. It was the independent entrepreneur, now an endangered species, from which the United States originally drew its strength.

With these kinds of changes, the logic for maintaining enormous information systems at great public expense, would rapidly fade. If the same money that government currently uses to "keep track of people" were simply used to pay those currently unemployed, to do productive work, the country would be on the road to recovery. One good example is the Immigration Service's millions spent on their massive computer network and "policing" functions. Again, this money spent directly for the betterment of the "Illegal alien" families that it presently terrorizes, would go a long way toward solving a lingering, serious social problem.

But now, the emphasis is on homogeneity . . . one nation, one culture, with no tolerance for divergent viewpoints, all legislated from a huge central government, and overseen by the world's largest law enforcement organization. It is a society, which while it lasts, serves only the power elite who endure administration after administration and control the mechanisms of government. It is these behind-the-scenes powers who benefit from "big government" with its unlimited data processing budgets.

It is a classic method of keeping the masses in line. By having its legislatures pass mountains of laws, the ruling powers can continue to justify its police agencies' Star-Wars computer networks tasked to enforce this incomprehensible infrastructure we loosely call American society.

The information networks with the FBI's leading the list, beyond routine police work, in large measure manage this function of superimposing the web of contrived and constantly changing legal structures upon the populace. It keeps the citizens sufficiently entangled and intimidated so as to dissipate any thoughts of major changes in government.

But, at this point, we encounter the paradox. We have a dangerous situation of public repression, which could lead to a social explosion unless major changes in government occur. And, at the same time, we have an overwhelmingly powerful government which uses a system of computer networks unique in the world, to impose a particularly repressive genre of "law and order", and which among other tasks, also protects and perpetuates itself by preventing major changes in government.

Where do we go from here? If there were really any quick and/or obvious solutions, they would have been implemented long ago. I have no doubt, oversimplified many of the issues presented. Make no mistake, they are NOT simple . . . neither the challenges, nor the answers. Most people search for win-win solutions to problems . . . some magic combination of factors where everyone lives happily ever after.

Situations involving entire cultures have never in history been that easy. Even when the Berlin Wall came down at one stroke, seemingly ending eastern Germany's ordeal, it was not quite that simple. In reality, most of a decade will pass before economic hardship evolves into western-style prosperity.

It is sincerely hoped that a civilized solution to this information-age totalitarianism will emerge. The Soviet Union found theirs. And aside from some years of financial turmoil, the only real damage has been to some die-hard communists and several million soldiers who, woke up one morning with no purpose in life. This kind of revolution we can live with.

The United States Government is just as arrogant as the former Soviet Government. But it is far more dangerous because it has enjoyed a measure of success. This by no means indicates that they got it all correct . . . merely that there is simply more right about the capitalism/ democracy model than the socialism/ communism model. It does however, unfortunately gives Uncle Sam the staying power to resist change.

Nonetheless, when one looks at the broad scale of time, EVERY MAJOR GOVERNMENT IN HISTORY HAS EVENTUALLY FALLEN. Some were conquered. Some rotted from within. Others were toppled by revolutions. Still others just faded away. Call it human nature, the law of entropy . . . whatever . . . the facts persist.

Hope can be found in this perspective. When confronted by the impenetrable fortress of the FBI with its ubiquitous computer tentacles, one can only pray for some kind of watershed event. What the future holds remains to be seen.

For the present, at an individual level, if you have ever lived in the United States, you can be virtually assured that the FBI has YOUR dossier on file. The 1992 tax laws included a change that requires babies to have their social security number assigned by their first birthday. This was the next to the last step in documenting the population. We can expect shortly, that the numbers will be issued with birth certificates.

The routine gathering of information by the government pervades all aspects of life . . . federally backed home mortgages, business loans, education, medical benefits, military and veterans affairs, taxes of course, various licenses, even something as innocuous as an application to go onto Federal land and cut a Christmas tree. EVERY TIME YOU INTERACT WITH THE GOVERNMENT IN ANY WAY WHATSOEVER, YOU GO INTO THE COMPUTER FILES. Then there are the state and local governments . . . and on and on.

Moreover, the FBI as we have just seen, has instant access to all of the civil and business information networks, such as credit reports, telephone companies, airline companies, utilities, and even private medical files. If a piece of information exists on a computer somewhere, the FBI can get at it . . . either directly or indirectly.

We can begin to see the new character of investigations. One tends to still think of the FBI agent with a trench coat and a submachine gun, going around blazing away at gangsters. Times have changed. The contemporary Special Agent is a expert in computerized data networks. He is specially trained in how the various public and private systems reflect the flow of information through American society. The majority of the work is done at his desk on a powerful workstation. If there is something that he can't get directly on the FBI files, he can request it from other networks.

The techniques are exceedingly efficient. It is no mystery at all that the FBI has constructed its computer empire. From their point of view, it is the most logical extension of their tools one could imagine. It is now a fact of life. Do not expect the situation to change without some fundamental change in philosophy of government.

Information is power.
Those who possess it, rule.
Those who do not, serve.

APPENDIX

JUSTICE/USA-999

SYSTEM NAME: Appendix of United States Attorneys' office locations:

Written requests for access to records in any of the following U.S. Attorneys' offices except the District of Columbia may be addressed to:

FOIA/Privacy Unit
Patrick Henry Building
601 D Street NW., Room 6410
Washington, D.C. 20530.

Requests for access to records in the District of Columbia may be addressed to:

FOIA/Privacy
United States Attorney's Office for the
District of Columbia
Judiciary Center Building
555 4th Street NW.
Washington, D.C. 20001.

Systems are located as listed below:

Alabama, N.
200 Federal Building
1800 Fifth Avenue North
Birmingham, Alabama 35203

Alabama, M.
500 Federal Building & Courthouse
15 Lee Street
Montgomery, Alabama 36104

Alabama, S.
169 Dauphin Street, Suite 200
Mobile, Alabama 36602

Alaska
Fed. Bldg. & U.S. Courthouse
Rm. C-253 222
West 7th Ave., 9
Anchorage
Alaska 99513

Arizona
4000 U.S. Courthouse
230 First Avenue
Phoenix, AZ 85025

Arkansas, E

331 P.O. & Courthouse Bldg.

600 West Capitol

Little Rock, Arkansas 72203

Arkansas, W

6th & Rogers

U.S. Post Office & Courthouse Bldg.

Fort Smith, Arkansas 72901

California, N

450 Golden Gate Avenue, Rm. 16201

San Francisco, Calif. 94102

California E

3305 Federal Building

650 Capitol Mall

Sacramento, Calif. 95814

California, C

312 N. Spring Street, Rm. 1306

Los Angeles, Calif. 90012

California, S

940 Front Street

Rm. 5-N-19

U.S. Courthouse

San Diego, Calif. 92189

Colorado

1961 Stout Street

Suite 1200-Drawer 3615

Federal Office Bldg.

Denver, Colorado 80294

Connecticut

United States Courthouse

141 Church Street

New Haven, Connecticut 06508

Delaware

J. Caleb Boggs Fed. Bldg.

844 King Street, Rm. 5110

Wilmington, Del. 19801

D.C.

Judiciary Center Bldg.

555 4th Street NW.

Washington, D.C. 20001

Florida, N

315 South Calhoun St.

Suite 510

Tallahassee, Florida 32301-1841

Florida, M

Robert Timberlake Bldg., Rm. 400

500 Zack Street

Tampa, Florida 33602

Florida, S

155 South Miami Avenue

Miami, Florida 33130

Georgia, N

Room 1800 Richard Russell Bldg.

75 Spring Street,

Atlanta, Georgia 30335

Georgia, M

Old. P.O. Bldg., Rm 303

Mulberry & 3rd Streets

Macon, Georgia 31202

Georgia, S

U.S. Courthouse, Room 237

125 Bull Street

Savannah, Georgia 31412

Guam

Suite 502-A Pacific News Building

238 Archbishop Flores St.

Agana, Guam 96910

Hawaii

Rm. C-242, PJKK Federal Bldg.

Box 50183, 300 Ala Moana Blvd.

Honolulu, Hawaii 96850

Idaho

Rm. 328 Federal Building

Box 037, 550 W Fort Street

Boise, Idaho 83724

Illinois, N

Everett McKinley Dirksen Bldg.

Rm. 1500 S. 219 S. Darborn Street

Chicago, Illinois 60604

Illinois, S

Rm. 330

750 Missouri Avenue

East St. Louis, Illinois 62201

Illinois, C

Rm. 312 Paul Findley Federal Bldg.

600 East Monroe Street

Springfield, Illinois 62701

Indiana N

4th Floor, Federal Building

507 State Street

Hammond, Ind. 46320

Indiana, S

U.S. Courthouse, Fifth Floor

40 E. Ohio Street

Indianapolis, Ind. 46204

Iowa, N

425 2nd Street S.E., Suite 950

The Center

Cedar Rapids, Iowa 52401

Iowa, S

115 U.S. Courthouse

E 1st & Walnut Streets

Des Moines Iowa 50309

Kansas

385 Federal Building

444 Quincy Street

Topeka, Kansas 66683

Kentucky, E

Fourth Floor

Federal Building

Limestone & Barr Streets

Lexington, Kentucky 40507

Kentucky, W

Bank of Louisville Bldg.

510 West Broadway, 10th Floor

Louisville, Kentucky 40202

Louisiana, E

Hale Boggs Fed. Bldg.

501 Magazine St., Rm. 210

New Orleans, LA 70130

Louisiana, M

339 Florida St., Sixth Floor

Baton Rouge, LA 70801 {PG 49151}

Louisiana, W

401 Edwards Street

Suite 1000

Shreveport, LA 71101-6133

Maine

East Tower-6th Floor

100 Middle Street Plaza

Portland, Maine 04101

Maryland

8th Floor U.S. Courthouse

101 W. Lombard Street

Baltimore, MD 21201

Massachusetts

1107 John W. McCormack Fed. Bldg.

USPO & Courthouse

Boston, Mass 02109

Michigan, E

817 Federal Building

231 W. Lafayette

Detroit, Michigan 46226

Michigan, W

Gerald R. Ford Federal Building &

U.S. Courthouse

110 Michigan St., N.W. Room 399

Grand Rapids, Michigan 49503

Minnesota

234 U.S. Courthouse

110 South 4th Street

Minneapolis, Minn. 55401

Mississippi N

Rm. 265 Federal Building

911 West Jackson Avenue

Oxford, Miss. 38655

Mississippi S

245 East Capitol St., Rm 324

Jackson, Miss. 39201

Missouri, E

Rm. 414, U.S. Court & Custom House

1114 Market Street

St. Louis, MO 63101

Missouri, W

549 U.S. Courthouse

811 Grand Avenue

Kansas City, MO 64106

Montana

316 N. 26th St.

Federal Bldg., Rm. 5043

Billings, Montana 59101

Nebraska

Room 8000, USPO & Courthouse,

Edward Zorinsky Federal Bldg.

215 N 17th Street

Omaha, Nebraska 68101

Nevada

701 E. Bridger Ave.

Suite 800

Las Vegas, Nevada 89101

New Hampshire

55 Pleasant Street, Rm. 439

Fourth Floor, Federal Bldg.

Concord, New Hampshire 03301

New Jersey

Federal Building

970 Broad Street, Rm. 502

Newark, N.J. 07102

New Mexico

625 Silver, S.W., 4th FL

Albuquerque, New Mex. 87102

New York, N

900 Federal Building

100 South Clinton Street

Syracuse, N.Y. 13260

New York, S

One St. Andrews Plaza

New York, N.Y. 10007

New York, E

U.S. Courthouse

225 Cadman Plaza

East Brooklyn, N.Y. 11201

New York, W

502 U.S. Courthouse

68 Court Street

Buffalo, N.Y. 14202

N. Carolina, E

Fourth Floor, Federal Building

310 New Bern Avenue

Raleigh, N.C. 27611

N. Carolina, M

L. Richardson Preyer Federal Building

324 West Market Street

Greensboro, N.C. 27402

N. Carolina, W

Rm 306, U.S. Courthouse

100 Otis Street

Asheville, N.C. 28802

N. Dakota

219 Federal Building

655 1st Avenue, North

Fargo, N.D. 58102

Ohio, N
Suite 500
1404 East Ninth Street
Cleveland, Ohio 44114

Ohio, S
Room 200
85 Marconi Boulevard
Columbus, Ohio 43215

Oklahoma, N
3600 U.S. Courthouse
333 West Fourth Street
Tulsa, Okla 74103

Oklahoma, E
333 Federal Courthouse & Office Bldg.
Fifth & Okmulgee
Muskogee, Okla 74401

Oklahoma, W
Room 4434
U.S. Courthouse & Fed. Office Bldg.
Oklahoma City, Okla 73102

Oregon
312 U.S. Courthouse
620 S.W. Main Street
Portland, Oregon 97205

Penn. E
3310 U.S. Courthouse
Independence Mall West
601 Market Street
Philadelphia, PA 19106

Penn. M
Suite 309, Federal Building
Washington & Linden Streets
Scranton, PA 18501

Penn. W
633 U.S.P.O. & Courthouse
7th Avenue & Grant Street
Pittsburgh, PA 15219

Puerto Rico
Rm. 101, Fed. Office Bldg.
Carlos E. Chardon Avenue
Hato Rey, P.R. 00918

Rhode Island
Westminister Square Building
10 Dorrance Street, Tenth Floor
Providence, R.I. 02903

South Carolina
Federal Building
1100 Laurel Street
Columbia, S.C. 29201

S. Dakota
135 Fed. Bldg., & U.S. Courthouse
400 S. Phillips Avenue
Sioux Falls, S.D. 57102

Tennessee, E
509 Main Street
Knoxville, TN 37901

Tennessee, M

Room 879, U.S. Courthouse

801 Broadway

Nashville, TN 37203-3870

Tennessee, W

1026 Fed. Office Bldg.

167 North Main Street

Memphis, TN 38103

Texas, N

310 U.S. Courthouse

10th & Lamar Streets

Ft. Worth, TX 76102

Texas, S

Courthouse & Federal Bldg.

515 Rusk Avenue, 3rd Floor

Houston, TX 77002

Texas, E

700 North Street, Suite 102

Beaumont, TX 77701

Texas, W

727 E. Durango Blvd.

Suite A-601

San Antonio, TX 78206

Utah

U.S. Courthouse, Room 476

350 South Main Street

Salt Lake City, UT 84101

Vermont

Federal Building

11 Elmwood Avenue, 6th Floor

Burlington, VT 05401

Virgin Islands

Federal Bldg., & U.S. Courthouse

Veterans Drive, Rm. 260

Charlotte Amalie

St. Thomas, V.I. 00802

Virginia, E

1101 King Street

Suite 502

Alexandria, VA 22314

Virginia, W

Room 456, Poff Federal Bldg.

210 Franklin Road, SW.

Roanoke, VA 24011

Washington, E

851 U.S. Courthouse

West 920 Riverside

Spokane, WA 99201

Washington, W

3600 Seafirst 5th Ave., Plaza

3800 Fifth Avenue

Seattle, WA 98104

West Virginia, N

Room 238, Federal Building

1125-1141 Chapline Street

Wheeling, WV 26003

West Virginia, S

Room 3201, Federal Building

500 Quarrier Street

Charleston, WV 25301

Wisconsin, E

330 Federal Building

517 East Wisconsin Avenue

Milwaukee, WI 53202

Wisconsin, W

120 N. Henry Street, Room 420

Madison, WI 53703

Wyoming

J.C. O'Mahoney Fed. Building

Room 4002, 2120 Capitol Avenue

Cheyenne, WV 82001

North Mariana Islands {PG 49152}

c/o U.S. Attorney's Office

6th Floor, Naura Bldg.

P.O. Box 377

Saipan, CM 96950